STOP COMPETING AND START WINNING: THE BUSINESS OF COACHING

BETH LAUNIERE AND LEO HOPF

IN ASSOCIATION WITH

THE AMERICAN VOLLEYBALL COACHES ASSOCIATION

(AVCA)

ISBN 978-1-7354993-0-7 Paperback

ISBN 978-1-7354993-1-4 Hardcover

ISBN 978-1-7354993-2-1 Audio

Library of Congress Control Number: 2020945281

Published by Mastery Publishing, USA

www.bethlauniere.com   www.leohopf.com

BIOS OF OUR EXPERTS

COACHES

John Dunning   (five-time NCAA volleyball champion and AVCA Hall of Famer, four-time National Coach of the Year, 16 years as head coach of the Stanford Cardinal, and 16 years as head coach of the Pacific Tigers)

Tom Farden   (head coach of the University of Utah Red Rocks gymnastics team and 2019 Pac-12 gymnastics Coach of the Year)

Tom Hilbert   (32 years as a Division One head volleyball coach and 12-time Mountain West Coach of the Year at Colorado State)

Jill Hirschinger   (40-year head volleyball coach and six-time America East Coach of the Year at the University of New Hampshire)

Amy Hogue   (13-year head softball coach at the University

of Utah and a second-team All-American as a player)

Tom Judson	(high school state champion softball coach)
Karch Kiraly	(coach of the USA women's national volleyball team, winner of the FIVB World Championship, three-time Olympic gold medalist as an athlete, and 146 professional beach volleyball titles)
Jamie Morrison	(former head coach of the Dutch women's national volleyball team and former assistant coach to both the USA men's and women's volleyball teams)
Urban Meyer	(won two national football BCS titles at the University of Florida and one national BCS title at The Ohio State University)
Terry Pettit	(coached Nebraska to its first volleyball national championship and won 21 conference championships in his 23 years as a coach)
Patti Tibaldi	(NAIA women's basketball Hall of Famer and retired head coach at Aquinas College)
Tara VanDerveer	(two-time women's basketball national champion at Stanford, member of the Naismith Memorial Basketball Hall of Fame, and coached USA women's national team to an Olympic gold medal)
Mary Wise	(three-time national volleyball Coach of the Year at Florida, 15-time SEC Coach of the Year, and winner of 18 consecutive SEC titles)

BUSINESS

Greg Cygan   (president of Heritage Oak Private School and volleyball club director)

Jay Debertin   (president and chief executive officer of the $32 billion Fortune 100 company CHS, the nation's leading farmer-owned cooperative and an agronomy, global energy, grains, and food company)

Jay Lund   (chairman of the board and chief executive officer of Andersen Corporation, America's premier window and door manufacturer, with locations in North America and Europe)

Tres Lund   (chief executive officer of Lund Food Holdings which owns and runs 27 upscale supermarkets in the Minneapolis-St. Paul metro area)

MEDICINE

Elizabeth M. Thackeray, MD

(University of Utah Anesthesiology Residency Program Director)

UTAH STAFF

Sheldon Carvalho (University of Utah volleyball director of operations)

Dan Corotan   (University of Utah volleyball assistant coach)

Malia Shoji   (University of Utah volleyball associate head coach)

FANS

Russ Franklin   (19-year Utah volleyball fan)

Sheila Franklin   (19-year Utah volleyball fan)

Harriet Hopf   (professor of anesthesiology and biomedical engineering at the University of Utah, executive coach, and Yale basketball, track, and softball alumna)

Steve Mirisola   (28-year Utah volleyball fan)

Anne Osborn, MD

(distinguished professor of radiology at the University of Utah and Stanford women's basketball and swimming alumna)

Lucy Osborn, MD

(former Associate Vice President for Health Sciences at the University of Utah and retired professor of pediatrics)

Russ Swonson   (P.A. announcer for the Utah volleyball team)

TABLE OF CONTENTS

LIST OF FIGURES

LIST OF TABLES

DEDICATION

Leo dedicates this book to the University of Utah athletes who have provided such wonderful entertainment and inspiration.

Beth dedicates this book to her current and former players, assistant coaches, and support staff with whom she has been in the trenches for thirty years. She also recognizes her competitors, both coaches and players, who were valiant in their many battles.

ACKNOWLEDGEMENTS

We would like to express our gratitude to the following people who graciously helped us develop and validate the ideas in this book:

- Kathy DeBoer and the American Volleyball Coaches Association (AVCA) for seeing the value of applying business principles to sport and for teaching young coaches that coaching is more than X's and O's. We also thank the AVCA for endorsing our book.

- Megan Kahn for inviting us to present the concepts in this book to members of the important coaching organization, WeCoach.

- Patti Tibaldi, NAIA women's basketball Hall of Famer and retired head coach at Aquinas College, who taught Beth the importance of empowering women through sport.

- Jill Hirschinger, former University of New Hampshire Volleyball Coach, for giving Beth her first college coaching job at Ferris State and instilling in her a passion for teaching young people.

- The late Mike Hebert, former University of Illinois Coach, who took a chance on a young assistant and taught her not just how to coach volleyball but how to build a program.

- Tom Judson, high school state champion softball coach, who taught Beth the meaning of Positive Mental Attitude (PMA).

- Greg Cygan, whose daughter played for Beth and who has continued his connection to the program long after she graduated. Greg's comments on each chapter rivaled the actual chapters in length.

- Harriet Hopf, who contributed greatly to our sections on feedback and diversity and who corrected grammar and added content for each chapter.

- Elaine Elliott, former Utah Women's Basketball Coach of 27 years, who was a mentor for Beth in her early years of coaching when a book like this did not exist.

- Joanna Reitz, who provided feedback from the perspective of a young coach on the way up.

Beth would like to acknowledge her family (parents Bob and Sally Launiere, siblings Steve, Scott, John, Tim, Julie, and Amy) and her many friends who have been by her side throughout her career, offering constant support while she built and maintained the Utah volleyball program for the past thirty years. What started as a program with one win the year before Beth arrived has turned into the nationally ranked Utah volleyball program that exists today.

Beth also acknowledges the individuals in the Utah Athletic Department, both past and present, who have supported and added value to her vision for 30 years. These include Chris Hill, Fern Gardner, Amy Hackett, Mary Bowman, Mark Harlan, Nona Richardson, Kyle Brennan, and Kate Charipar.

We would like to thank our beta readers who contributed their expertise and time to make this a better book. Our beta readers were Kathy DeBoer, Tom Farden, Jill Hirschinger, Harriet Hopf, Allison Ivetic, Julie Launiere, Kim Maroon, Jamie Morrison, Berkeley Oblad, Joanna Reitz, and Patti Tibaldi. All errors are our own.

We thank Emma Love for narrating the audiobook, aksaramantra for our cover design, Vanessa Maynard for typesetting, and Yasmin Sara Gruss for proofreading. Finally, we would like to thank our editor, Wes Cowley, for his many suggestions and corrections.

OVERVIEW

The pairing of a business consultant with a Division I head coach may seem unusual, but management consulting has many lessons to bring to coaching. Conversations between friends connected by their love of volleyball developed into innovative ideas about how coaches can run the "business" component of their program, stay connected with their players, and elevate their team's success.

Over the past five years, the authors have worked together to bring select concepts and tools from the world of business into the University of Utah's volleyball program. We have presented our approach to numerous coaches' groups, and, based on the positive feedback from coaches at all levels, we decided to write this book.

Many coaches share a similar career trajectory. They started as players, entered coaching as a volunteer assistant or as a director of operations, earned promotion to assistant coach, and, were eventually hired into a head coaching role. What they learned along the way depended on who they had to learn from. If they were fortunate to learn from great thinkers and communicators, they were well prepared when their turn came to run a program. If they had less capable teachers, they learned through trial and error and repeated the mistakes of those before them.

But no matter how effective the coaches were that they trained under, most of their lessons came from inside the world of their sport. Because of this, many coaches have similar bodies of knowledge. A given coach may be better or worse than their competition, but they are all drawing from the same storehouse of ideas.

Winning as a coach requires incorporating ideas wherever you can find them and blending those which make sense into your program to make it more effective and more efficient. If you can access relevant ideas and tools from outside of coaching (whether from business, politics, healthcare, education, volunteer work, or other fields), you will provide yourself with lasting competitive advantages.

You will need to carefully sift and tailor these ideas to make sure they are relevant to coaching in general and to your program in particular. But if you do so, you will find many ideas and tools that can help improve your program in both the short and long term and that will provide depth to the experience for yourself, your staff, and your players.

This book will address questions such as:

- What does it take to design a program to win consistently, year after year?
- How can you set clear expectations so you realize full value from your star performers and deal appropriately with your "C" performers?
- How can you delegate effectively so the right work gets done by the right people in the right way?
- How should you manage and develop a staff that will

deliver results and that will free up the head coach to do the things only they can do?

· How should you optimize staff interactions on both short-term tasks and longer-term projects?

· How can you assess each of your player's capabilities, growth, and eventual ceilings so you can plan to fill gaps and leverage their particular strengths?

· How can you lead a program remotely during a crisis, such as the COVID-19 pandemic, and afterward, when things have evolved into a new normal?

· How can you look ahead and make sure your program is prepared for the future rather than being stuck in the past?

To validate the concepts in this book, the authors interviewed top coaches in both men's and women's sports. These interviews include John Dunning (five NCAA volleyball national championships), Tara VanDerveer (two NCAA basketball national championships and one Olympic gold medal), and Karch Kiraly (head coach of the United States women's national volleyball team and three-time Olympic gold medalist as an athlete). The insights and quotes from these luminaries run throughout the book.

We also interviewed four business CEOs to provide ideas from their organizations that are relevant to leading athletic organizations. Their comments are used throughout the book as well, adding richness from beyond the normal boundaries of athletics.

This is a book for athletic directors, administrators, coaches, and staff in all sports. But since the ideas are transferrable to many different fields, it can also be used as a business book. The book describes approaches and strategies to design programs that will not just compete hard but will win at a high-level year after year. If you are early in your career, the concepts and tools will provide a template showing what you must learn to succeed. If you are more experienced, you will find new ideas that can bring your leadership and management to a new level.

Athletics is a people-focused activity, and many of the ideas that work in sports are transferrable to other fields such as business, medicine, education, and the arts. And since athletics is seen as the gold standard for instilling passion, those in other fields can learn how to inspire and motivate their individuals and teams from those who are the very best at it.

This book explores the intersection of athletics and business, and will provide lasting advantages for those willing to look beyond traditional boundaries.

ABOUT BETH LAUNIERE: BETHLAUNIERE@GMAIL.COM

Beth Launiere enters her 31st season at the helm of the University of Utah volleyball program in 2020 and is coming off one of the most successful seasons in the program's history.

Launiere was named the Pac-12 Coach of the Year in 2019 after leading Utah to a 24-10 record, a third-place finish in the Pac-12 and the program's fourth Sweet 16 appearance (two in the last three years), with four players named to the All-American team. Along with earning her first Pac-12 Coach of the Year honor, she also was named the AVCA West Region Coach of the Year for the fourth time (2001, '06, '08, '19). She had been named the Mountain West Conference (MWC) Coach of the Year three times (2004, '06, '08).

Beth is a past president of the American Volleyball Coaches Association (AVCA). She has also coached in the USA National Team program for the past 11 years.

ABOUT LEO HOPF: TEAMHOPF@GMAIL.COM

First and foremost, Leo is a volleyball fan. He connected with Beth through fan club events. He and his wife joined Beth and her team for a two-week European tour, during which they began the conversations which led to this book.

Leo Hopf is the co-author of *Rethink, Reinvent, Reposition: 12 Strategies to Renew Your Business and Boost Your Bottom Line*, which was named the book of the month in July 2010 by the Institute for Management Studies. He has led strategy efforts in 15 countries and in 40 different industries. He earned a Master of Business Administration degree with highest distinction from the Tuck School of Business at Dartmouth and has bachelor's degrees in chemical engineering and in metallurgical engineering from the University of Minnesota. He has led hundreds of strategy sessions with CEOs, leadership teams, and boards of directors, and he designed the decision-making and strategic-planning processes for five of the Fortune 100 largest companies.

CHAPTER 1: THE PERFECT MATCH

"Every volleyball coach recruits and trains and prays for a night like @UtahVolleyball had vs BYU yesterday. The closest thing to a flawless match (for Utah) that I have seen in years. Every player hitting on all cylinders - a thing of beauty. BYU had no chance. Kudos Utah."

Tweet from Mark C. Massey, Head Volleyball Coach,
University of Puget Sound

"Whoever, wherever, whatever it takes."
Utah volleyball motto, 2019 NCAA tournament

The match had just ended, and the bright red of celebrating Utah fans covered the floor, singing along to the Utah pep band's continuous repeat of the fight song, punctuated each time by a deafening chorus of "Go Utes!" The announcers grabbed the Utah stars for their TV interviews. Utah was headed to the 2019 Sweet

16 after defeating in-state rival BYU 25-15, 25-15, 25-15, in the closest thing to a perfect match Beth has ever had in her 30-year career.

The 3,250 fans at BYU's Smith Fieldhouse had just witnessed what can happen when everything comes together in a flawless moment. Of course, the nearly 3,000 fans in the home blue and white of the BYU Cougars were not celebrating. But 300 red-clad, die-hard Utah fans had driven the 45 minutes between the two schools, and their voices filled the arena. BYU had entered the match as the favorite: they were higher ranked and had defeated Utah the last several times they had met.

But as those in blue and white quietly filed out, the Utah band played on. The Utah players emerged from the locker room doused in water, shoulders covered in ice, and smiles lighting up their faces, and the party in red continued. Evidently, the Utah fans couldn't take the hint and wouldn't leave until the workers began turning off the lights in the fieldhouse. The celebration was just too sweet!

This was Utah's Perfect Match, but it was not a fluke in which everything just happened to come together for one night. This match was the result of a team that had been designed to win and that had perfectly executed its plan.

UTAH'S 2019 NCAA DRAW

It is always tempting to complain about your draw in the tournament. But in the 2019 NCAA tournament, the Utes may have had a point.

Utah had hoped to host the first two rounds given its RPI and record. But they just missed on hosting and instead were assigned to travel to BYU for the Provo Regional. In the first round, they would face Illinois, a team that had made the NCAA Final Four the year before and had a couple of key players back from injury. If Utah were to win in the first round, they would most probably face BYU in the second round. BYU had also been in the 2018 Final Four. And should Utah make it past BYU, they were most likely headed to the Stanford Regional to meet the defending national champions on their home court. The NCAA had asked the Utes to beat three teams in a row from the previous year's Final Four, which would be no easy task.

Rather than focus on the perceived unfairness of the draw, the staff and team adopted a motto that inspired them to feed off the slight and the opportunity: "Whoever, wherever, whatever it takes."

Tom Judson, high school state champion softball coach, addressed this attitude when he said:

> "I always used this motivation with every really good championship caliber team I have ever coached. You always think, as you are progressing through the tournament, that you will run into one truly great team that could beat everyone else. Well, just maybe WE ARE THAT TEAM!"

ROUND ONE: ILLINOIS

Illinois came into the match on a hot streak, having won four of their last five Big Ten conference matches. They had suffered a rash of injuries early in the year, which had lowered their ranking and their seed, but were back at full strength coming into the NCAA tournament.

Utah won the first set but lost the next two and were trailing the Fighting Illini late in the fourth set. Utah rallied and then kept the pressure on to win a long five-set match.

At one critical juncture late in the fourth set, Utah was in desperate need of a point and a momentum change. Middle blocker Berkeley Oblad was serving and playing back row. Late in the rally, it appeared Utah would have to free ball it over because the ball had been saved deep in the court. Instead, Oblad literally pushed aside the outside hitter, took a hard swing from the back row, and got the kill for the point. From that moment, Utah took control of the match. "Whoever, wherever, whatever it takes," indeed. After the match, Beth tweeted:

> "It was the single most inspirational play I've ever been involved with in my 30 years."

ROUND TWO: PREPARING FOR BYU

BYU has a great program, and their crowds in the Smith Fieldhouse give them an incredible home court advantage. Utah and BYU play each other every year, and the staff and players have a tremendous amount of knowledge of and respect for each other. The fans of the rivalry, on the other hand, do not have much love lost between them, and the magnitude of this match was felt by all. BYU had swept Utah out of the NCAA tournament the year before and had beaten Utah in the regular season in each of the previous three years.

In contrast to Utah's brutal five-set match against the Fighting Illini, BYU had a relatively short first-round match against the New Mexico State Aggies. BYU won in straight sets, hit .386 for the match, served eight aces, and had a remarkable 16-0 scoring run.

Before the BYU match, the conversation amongst the Utah fans was about how the long match the night before would affect the team. The Illinois match had been difficult and emotional, and the Utah fans were worried that BYU would come out fresh while Utah would come out tired.

Inside the Utah locker room, however, the story was entirely different. There was a universal feeling of calm and confidence. Beth said very little to the team as there was no need. The night before, after the long-fought battle with Illinois, Beth told her team to get some rest and "we will worry about BYU tomorrow." She and her staff met back at the hotel but decided they already knew the Cougars well enough and that less was going to be more when it came to scout preparation.

The next day, the team did a light serve and pass at the gym and went back to the hotel for a meal and a short 30-minute review session. There was a sense of not needing to do a lot of talking; they knew what they had to do. Rather than being nervous about the chance of making the Sweet Sixteen, the staff and coaches were relaxed and ready. They knew they had been preparing themselves for moments such as these, and the players felt that a loss would be unacceptable.

The staff and players saw the upcoming match as the culmination of the last five years of planning and hard work. The thought of a season-ending loss was not in anyone's head. The staff and players had committed to doing something the program had never done before, and the feeling amongst the players was that they would be shocked if they were to lose. Everything was ready and there was no need to make things more complex. As Tara VanDerveer, Stanford women's basketball coach, told us:

"Coaching is not rocket science – Keep it simple."

ROUND TWO: UTAH DEFEATS BYU
IN THE PERFECT MATCH

The crowd was loud as match time approached, but the dominant sound was the Utah pep band. They had turned out in full force, and BYU's band was elsewhere. There were two patches of red in the sea of blue and white. The largest was in the stands behind the Utah bench and a smaller group sat directly across the floor.

Utah began the first set with an ace and built a 9-2 lead. Their five blocks and .433 hitting percentage quickly ended the set. The second set began tighter but ended with the same 25-15 score. In the third set, Utah once again jumped out to a 9-2 lead and finished the match with the third 25-15 score of the night.

Other than 0-0, Utah was never tied in the match, and never trailed. The Utes came out on the attack and never looked back. BYU had only a single run of three points in the entire match. Utah sided out at over 80%, so it was almost impossible for BYU to catch up. The combination of Utah siding out at an astounding rate and going on small and large runs all night long was a lethal combination for the Cougars.

Utah passed beautifully, the setting was on point, and they hit aggressively from both the front and back rows. In virtually every long rally, Utah had BYU back on their heels. BYU would play strong defense and get the ball back over, but then Utah would attack again and again until the point had been won. They were relentless.

BYU had been swept at home for the first time in nearly a decade. But the reaction from the Utah staff and players was neither shock nor surprise. Instead, it was excitement and satisfaction in knowing they had perfectly executed what had been designed to win. There was no arrogance in the team, just a deep feeling of confidence that they were ready for the upcoming Stanford match in the Sweet 16.

Figure 1-1: The payoff of the Perfect Match and being designed to win

COMMENTS FROM FANS WHO ATTENDED THE PERFECT MATCH

The Utah fans who attended the Perfect Match immediately recognized they had seen a moment they would treasure. Russ and Sheila Franklin said:

> "The BYU match was truly the most flawless match that we have seen in our 19 seasons as Utah fans."

Steve Mirisola said:

> "Going back to the first weekend of the past season, it was evident that the team was breathing fire, and that same attitude carried all the way through to the NCAA tournament."

Anne Osborn summed up the BYU match this way:

> "It was the most exciting, delicious, and glorious athletic experience I have ever had, as either a player or a fan."

The most touching reaction came from an avid Utah fan who was in the 3rd grade. She had brought a large Utah sign to the match and boldly sat in the BYU student section directly behind the service line. This is how her mother described what her daughter told her (we have translated it into first person so it reads as she would have described it):

> "I was really nervous when we went in because I knew I wanted the team to know I was there for them. The day before, a security person said the student section was open and anyone could sit there. When we walked in, I was really excited and I wanted to sit there because the Utes deserved fans there too. People weren't nice to me, but I didn't care, I ignored them. The Ute players saw me sitting there with my big Utah sign and they would wave and smile at me. My sisters kept checking on me, but I was ok. I wasn't afraid. I was just proud to sit there so they knew I was there for them. My mom also told me it might be the last time I would get to see Berkeley Oblad play, and I just didn't want to cry. I feel like I helped the Utes win and supported them. I want to be just like them."

Can you think of a better example of the power of sports to influence the life of a young fan? You may now take a moment to dry your eyes.

PREPARING FOR STANFORD
IN THE SWEET SIXTEEN

Stanford was the defending national champion and was ranked number three in the country. But the main reason they were ranked that low was that two-time national Player of the Year Kathryn Plummer had missed over one-third of their matches due to injury. Utah and Stanford had met in two tightly contested conference matches with Stanford defeating Utah 3-2 at home and 3-1 at Utah.

Stanford had won 13 straight matches and had not lost a set in the first two rounds of the NCAA tournament. But rather than feeling intimidated, Utah felt confident. As evidence of this, one of Utah's fans had made a sign in the preseason predicting Utah's record. He gave it to Beth, who happily posed with his predicted record.

Figure 1-2: Beth Launiere holding prediction from preseason.

Going into the Stanford match, Utah had 24 wins and 9 losses. The week of the regional semifinal match, one of the players reminded Beth of the sign and said that the prediction of 24-10 was NOT going to be correct. That would put the team losing at Stanford. Neither the Utah staff nor players were ready to end the season.

ROUND THREE: THE SWEET SIXTEEN VS. STANFORD

Utah jumped off to a lead with a 25-22 victory in the first set. Stanford roared back with dominant 25-14, 25-10 victories in sets two and three. Rather than crumbling, however, Utah turned the tables in set four and routed Stanford 25-12. Malia Shoji, University of Utah volleyball associate head coach, described the team's attitude that allowed them to come back in the fourth set when many teams would have simply felt good about putting up a strong showing. She said:

> "When the players came into the timeouts, they were participating, giving ideas, and totally present. They had been beaten up in sets two and three and that is not how they were going to end the season. They dug deep and proved themselves in their dominant set four performance."

The fifth set started out with one of the Utah players crashing into the bench and losing her breath. After a one-minute delay, she said she was ok and went back onto the court and got the next kill. The resilience she demonstrated during that minute, and that her teammates had demonstrated all match long, was a skill that had been ingrained in them by the coaches. Utah was going to fight to the end.

The set started out close, but Stanford went on a run to open up a lead and took the final set 15-11. Stanford went on to win the national title and no other team in the tournament took even a single set off of them. Utah had lost but had pushed the eventual champions in an impressive fashion.

REACTION AFTER THE LOSS TO STANFORD

The team's reaction after the loss to Stanford was most enlightening. They had been so dialed in on each and every point that they were actually surprised the match had ended and that they had lost and their season was over. They had been totally focused on their mission and purpose and not on winning or losing.

This is the mark of a team designed to win. Being designed to win doesn't mean you will always win. It means that you put yourself and your team in the position to win and that your focus will be on how you play and improve rather than on the end result.

After Stanford won the national championship, Stanford head coach Kevin Hambly told the media that Utah had given them the toughest test of the tournament, including the two teams they beat in the Final Four.

COMMENTS FROM OTHER COACHES

Utah's playoff run caught the imagination of coaches around the country. At the American Volleyball Coaches Association (AVCA) convention at the Final Four in Pittsburgh, Beth was pulled aside time and again by coaches who had seen something different and special in Utah's play. The most common comments were:

- Your team plays so aggressively and with so much passion. We loved watching them play.
- Your back-row attack is one of the best in the county.
- It was impressive how you found room for two lefties to play. And since both were named All-Americans, having a left-handed outside and a left-handed opposite was clearly a key to the team's success.

WHAT LED TO THE PERFECT MATCH?

The Perfect Match against BYU and the rest of the playoff run didn't come out of nowhere. Hard work from long before the matches laid the groundwork for winning.

All year long, the team focused on being 2% better. Just 2%. With the parity in collegiate volleyball today amongst the best schools, 2% is enough to turn a loss into a win. The team created their slogan of "2gether" to incorporate the idea of the 2% improvement.

In the past, the team had done individual and team goal setting at the start of the fall season so that incoming players could participate. But in 2019, they set their goals in the spring with the thought that setting the right goals would take time and should not be rushed. The team decided that the newcomers would just need to buy into the goals when they arrived on campus.

The team didn't rush the conversations in the spring. They spent 20–30 hours in team meetings and at least 20 hours in leadership meetings. In these conversations, they dove deep into concepts and built a solid understanding of what the team and individuals would need do in the fall if they were going to fulfill their mission of "doing something the Utah volleyball program had never done before." The team interpreted this statement to mean getting to the Elite Eight or Final Four or to win a National Championship. Once the team mission had been chosen, the coaches made sure everyone set tangible and understandable goals that would contribute to the overall success of the program.

The Perfect Match was the result of a program designed to win. How to design your program to win will be the topic for the rest of this book.

MAIN POINTS IN THIS CHAPTER

- Having a program designed to win means not being surprised by success.
- Program victories come from both team and individual training, focus, and heroics.
- Your wins inspire others, both coaches and fans.

CHAPTER 2: WHAT IT MEANS TO BE DESIGNED TO WIN

"If your program is designed to win, there is an expectation of excellence that cannot be satisfied with just beating teams you should defeat."

Patti Tibaldi (NAIA Women's Basketball Hall of Fame)

In this book, we will clarify the differences between programs that simply compete hard and those that are designed to win. Along the way, we will give you the tools and concepts you need to design your program to win so you will enjoy consistent success, improved job security, and enhanced professional opportunities.

In programs that are simply competing hard, coaches and support staff go to work every day and do their best. They scramble, deal with the issues of the day, and fight fires as they arise. There are unending demands on their time and never a chance to step back and plan. Their world is reactive, and the pressure unending. They work hard every day, but they are not necessarily working smart.

If a program that simply competes hard happens to have great players, they win. If they have a year with only average players, they lose. Annual success is highly variable, and each year seems like a roll of the dice.

Coaches and staff in programs designed to win experience things quite differently. Success is embedded in their culture and their processes. Leaders have time to think and to proactively and creatively address challenges. Everyone works hard, of course, but their work is more effective and is made easier by the advantages their design provides.

As Tara VanDerveer, two-time NCAA women's basketball national champion, said:

"You need to be laser focused on being a great team."

CHARACTERISTICS OF PROGRAMS THAT ARE DESIGNED TO WIN

Programs that are designed to win have the following characteristics:

- A clear, compelling, and positive vision of what the program is designed to accomplish—a vision understood by everyone and that guides their actions and decision-making (this chapter).
- A growth mindset that enables coaches, support staff, and players to consistently improve their skill set, incorporate new concepts, and keep themselves fresh and prepare for the future (this chapter). As Karch Kiraly, coach of the USA women's national volleyball team, put it,

"You have to have a ruthless and never-ending pursuit of mastery."

- High expectations for everyone in the program so that stars reach their full potential and "C" performers are improved or removed (Chapter 3).
- Effective delegation so that the right work is done by the right people and the program is aligned from top to bottom (Chapter 4).
- Clear givens and quality commitments to ensure everyone understands what is being asked of them for both tasks and projects (Chapter 5).
- High-quality coaches and support staff members who are lifelong learners, open to mentorship, and hungry to be part of a program designed to win (Chapter 6).
- Tools for finding the right people to bring on to your staff and for bringing them quickly up to speed (Chapter 7).
- A roster of players that fulfill necessary team roles and who are developed to reach their individual potentials (Chapter 8).
- A recognition of the value and engagement of fans and donors (Chapter 9).
- The ability to run the program effectively both in normal conditions and remotely during a crisis such as that caused by the COVID-19 pandemic (Chapter 10).
- A continuous focus on preparing for the future rather than being stuck in the past (Chapter 11).
- The leadership style and capabilities that tie everything together (Chapter 12).
- The willingness to implement new ideas and take the first steps, even if they are small (Chapter 13).

Designing your program to win takes focus, effort, and commitment. Beth knew she was in for a challenge when the University of Utah entered the Pac-12 in 2011. She wasn't just satisfied with being competitive in one of the best volleyball conferences in the country, she wanted to win.

BUILDING A PROGRAM DESIGNED TO WIN

Just before Utah entered the Pac-12, its volleyball program was operating at a high level as a member of the Mountain West Conference. The Utes were typically at or near the top of the conference, and Beth and her players had won numerous conference and national awards and honors. Overall, life was good.

Utah had one year from the announcement to prepare for entry into the Pac-12. Beth immediately began seeking advice from coaches who were in that conference and the Big Ten, as well as from coaches from other schools who had reached the NCAA Final Four.

To compete and win, Beth would need to improve all aspects of Utah's program. If the Utes simply competed hard, they would fall short of the top teams. For that matter, if they simply competed hard, they would fall short of the middle teams in the Pac-12 as well.

Beth made the choice to tear apart every aspect of her program and build it back up, incorporating every improvement, both large and small, she could find. This was what it would take to move from simply competing hard to being designed to win. But, where to start? What to prioritize? How to deal with the current program while trying to design the new program?

These were the questions Beth faced as she made the transition and redesigned her team to win. The lessons she learned from meeting these challenges gave rise to many of the ideas in this book.

This was not the first change Beth had encountered during her career. When she began as a head coach at age 26, she had a simple organization with only four people reporting to her. The Utah volleyball organization chart at that time looked like this:

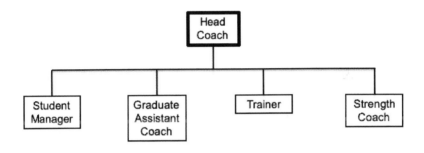

Figure 2-1: Beth's first org chart as head coach

At this stage, there was no need for management because there were only a few coaches and support staff and they met with each other and the players every day. Her challenge at that time was learning how to do her own job and improve her coaching skills. Since the organization was small, she could spend most of her time with her players and be involved in their lives both inside and outside of athletics.

As John Dunning, American Volleyball Coaches Association Hall of Famer, said about his early career:

"I had little staff and had done everything essentially on my own early in my career. I had been programmed to think I could do it all myself. I had to change my thinking on how I did things in order to have time to grow my program."

Over time, Utah's program grew. By the time she was coaching in the Mountain West Conference, her organization had evolved:

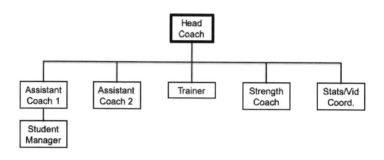

Figure 2-2: Beth's org chart in the Mountain West

Now, Beth not only had to be a coach, but she also had to learn how to lead and develop young coaches. This included training her staff on skills and systems so their own teaching was consistent; on the nuts and bolts of working in an office environment; on professionalism; and, with young assistants in particular, on how to build appropriate relationships with players and other staff members.

For the first time, Beth could no longer be involved with everything herself. When she began as a head coach, she had been a coach. Now she was both a coach and a manager. And, though coaching was what she loved and what enabled her to be creative and innovative, her management responsibilities kept growing and demanding more of her time.

Entering the Pac-12 increased expectations and the Utah volleyball program quickly expanded in complexity. As it entered the Pac-12, the need for more staff arose and the program looked like this:

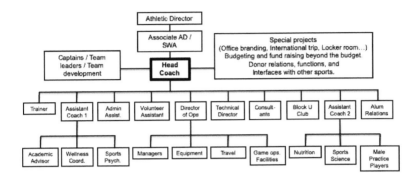

Figure 2-3: Beth's org chart on entering the Pac-12

Beth knew she needed to do something different if she was going to successfully transition the Utah volleyball program into the Pac-12 and keep it as a nationally competitive program. The path would look different from her early years as a coach, but the principles and foundation of the program would remain the same.

But it wouldn't be easy. In their first two years competing in the Pac-12, Utah volleyball finished in 9th place and lost almost three times as many conference matches as they won.

MANAGEMENT DEMANDS TAKE TIME AWAY FROM COACHING

The program was now so complex that management took up all of Beth's time and then some. Rather than feeling like a coach, she began to feel like the general manager of a small business. Problems arose from every direction and the demands on her time never let up. With more layers between Beth and her players, and with the support staff having most of the touchpoints with the players, she began to feel distanced from her team. And, though she has a business degree, Beth never signed up to be a manager. She signed up to be a coach, and it no longer felt like she was doing much of that.

Even after spending a year "overturning every stone" to look for ways to improve, Utah was still just competing hard. There was no time to plan and no clear changes that would make things better. As Sheila Franklin, a long-time Utah volleyball fan, said:

> "There were growing pains when we entered the Pac-12. We remember rooting for hitting double figures in sets against the elite teams during the first few seasons."

Beth's life was now filled with thoughts such as these:

- I feel like I am the metal ball in a pinball game reacting to the bumpers and flippers.
- I am spending virtually all of my time with coaches and support staff, and almost none with my players.
- I know I should delegate, but it is faster and easier to do it myself.
- Sometimes when I do delegate, the work is not done correctly or on time, and it is still my responsibility.

The situation came to a head after a lopsided loss to Stanford. As she debriefed with her assistants and players, the cause of the loss became clear and undeniable. Stanford was just better than Utah in virtually every way. There was no way to sugar coat it to make it more palatable. Everyone in the room agreed the team needed to get better. And, it became clear they needed to go farther than they thought and it would take longer than they had expected.

THE POWER OF A LASTING
VISION STATEMENT

Programs that are designed to win have a clear and unchang-ing vision statement that guides choices and actions at all levels. Without such a statement, it is easy to lose sight of the big picture when day-to-day demands become overwhelming.

Beth's vision statement has remained nearly unchanged for three decades and distills her philosophy into three short, yet meaningful, statements:

- Win at the highest level.
- Learn lifelong lessons and become a lifelong learner.
- Have a team that loves, trusts, and respects each other.

Beth has gone back and forth on using the word "love" in re-gard to her team. She explains to her team that love refers to de-veloping a deep and authentic relationship that is honest, healthy, and productive. Even if this did not lead directly to winning (and you could easily argue that it does), it certainly helps the players, coaches, and support staff have a more meaningful and enjoyable experience.

A vision statement that is just framed and sits on the wall does nothing. To be of value, the statement must be understood by all and must guide their choices and actions. For this to be the case, the vision statement must first be clear and specific enough that it can be tied to all of the program's activities and, second, be internalized by everyone.

The first part of Beth's vision statement is to win at the highest level. Every coach wants to win, but what does it mean to win at the highest level? For Beth's program at Utah, it means finishing

at the top of the Pac-12 and competing for a national championship. Your program may have a different definition of winning.
What matters is that your definition is clear and shared by all.

Relevant factors in deciding what winning means for your program include:

- At what level are you competing? (Professional, Power 5,
  NCAA Division 1, Division 2, Division 3, NAIA, Club,
  High School.)
- What is your program's current status? (Are you currently
  at the high end of your program's historic performance,
  in the middle, or at the low end?)
- What is your program's trajectory? (On the rise, in
  decline, or spinning your wheels?)
- How well is your program financed, and what are your
  athletic department's goals for your program?

Your definition of winning should be a stretch but it should
still be attainable. If you set your definition of winning too high,
you will experience failure year after year. If you set it too low, you
will meet your target, but may never reach the heights you could
have achieved with a more aggressive and inspirational goal.

The second part of Beth's vision statement is to learn lifelong
lessons and become a lifelong learner through the experience of
winning at the highest level. The greatest lessons are learned in
the pursuit of excellence: when you are challenged on a daily
basis and forced to grow and get better or get beat. It is in those
uncomfortable times that you learn the most about yourself.

As Malia Shoji, University of Utah volleyball associate head
coach, said:

"Becoming a lifelong learner to me is one of the best life lessons we learn in the program."

Early in her career, Beth had a small coaching and support staff and was able to spend significant amounts of time with her players. When asked, she was able to provide help in all aspects of their lives, whether it be athletic, academic, personal, or otherwise. Interactions and discussions between Beth and her players about life happened organically and informally. But, as her program became more complex, there were more and more people between her and her players.

Many of these were specialists, including academic advisors, trainers, strength coaches, mental health professionals, and nutritionists, who addressed specific areas of players' collegiate athletic lives that Beth herself had once overseen. This led to Beth's realization that she could still teach lifelong lessons, but those lessons would need to be taught primarily in the context of volleyball rather than other aspects of her players' lives.

The learning process became more intentional and more professional in a very positive way. It soon became clear that the lessons the athletes needed to learn were different for the different classes. First years and sophomores tended to need simpler life lessons, while juniors and seniors tended to need career-oriented and more complex lessons to prepare for their life after collegiate volleyball. Teaching these lessons benefits the players and brings joy to the coaches as they witness their players grow and mature.

The third part of Beth's vision statement is to love, trust, and respect each other. This seems like it could be simply a statement of her personal belief of how people should interact with each other. But, if you are going to build a winning team, you need to have everyone heading in the same direction.

Realizing this third part is never easy, but it may be easier at the university level than it is at the high school or club level. At the university level, the athletes are living on their own for the first time and there is a natural shift from relying on their family to relying on their teammates and coaches. This shift provides the foundation for building a team that loves, trusts, and respects each other.

Coaches develop each of their players to their highest potential, but since their ceilings vary, issues of playing time and roles on the team are unavoidable. These issues tend to rear their heads at the most inopportune of times, and they can lead to difficult conversations between the players, coaches, and the support staff. Dealing with these potential conflicts is much easier and less distracting if you start from a position of love, trust, and respect.

One other benefit of this third part of Beth's vision is that it fosters risk taking. A productive practice environment is one in which a player feels safe to make mistakes and experience failure while still feeling supported throughout the process.

AUTHENTICITY IS A REQUIREMENT OF BEING DESIGNED TO WIN

To be authentic, you must develop a deep understanding of who you are and what you believe. Once you have distilled these truths, you must be able to express them in different ways to different audiences, including players, staff, administrators, parents, and fans. You will present different versions of yourself to each of these audiences, but each version must be consistent with what you know to be true.

Coaching is a profession that stretches you as a person on a daily basis. You will frequently be faced with challenging situations requiring solutions for which you may not have the answers, and that puts you in a vulnerable position. Your decisions and actions affect people's lives, especially those who are young, impressionable, and looking to you for insight. In these situations, it is critical that you have a level of authenticity so that they can focus on what you are saying rather than wondering if what you are saying is what you actually believe.

Even totally authentic leaders have private areas of their lives they choose not to share with others. Perhaps you made mistakes as a youth that you now look back upon with shame. And maybe, even now, you are involved in activities that you love, but that others might not appreciate. For example, you may have amassed a vast collection of miniature porcelain farm animals, or you may have decorated yourself with tattoos that are not normally visible while wearing street clothes. It is up to you whether you make these public or keep them to yourself. What is critical is that when you choose to speak or take actions that are visible to the public, they are consistent with your core truths.

As you consider what to reveal or keep private, remember the power of vulnerability as eloquently expressed by Brené Brown in her book, *Dare to Lead.* If you always present yourself as perfect, it will be hard for those around you to admit they are not. If you make yourself vulnerable by revealing your youthful mistakes or the extent of your porcelain collection, you may inspire others to be courageous and authentic themselves. It is okay for your players or staff to see you make mistakes as long as you own up to them and make the appropriate corrections.

Authenticity can be misused as an excuse to be dismissive, unkind, or cruel to others. "That's just who I am, get used to it," you might say, explaining away your inappropriate or unprofessional behavior as being true to yourself. You may have strongly held beliefs that you feel you must impose on others whether they like it or not. But that is not authenticity, it is bullying.

You can't fake authenticity. Trying to tell each audience what you think they want to hear will expose you as someone who can't be trusted and doesn't deserve to be followed. Being true to who you are is always the best answer.

THE HUNGER TO WIN

Coaches may express it differently, but if you are going to win at the highest level, you need a hunger to win. There will be many opportunities to slack off or let things slide. There will be times when it would feel so much easier to just give up. It is the staff and players who keep getting up after being knocked down that will come out on top.

Tom Hilbert, 12-time Mountain West volleyball Coach of the Year at Colorado State, summarized it this way:

> "When two great teams face each other and the game elements are even, it can be the competitive drive that sets one team apart."

Urban Meyer, winning coach of three football BCS national championships, believes the hunger to win comes from inside. He told us:

> "There is one common denominator among elite players, coaches, and executives, and that is an elite competitive spirit. A refuse-to-lose mentality. As I moved along my coaching journey that became the

number one criterion I would look for in recruiting and hiring a coach."

IDENTIFYING AND OVERCOMING ROADBLOCKS

Teams designed to win look ahead to what they will need to do to achieve their goals. Whether it be to win against your historic rival, to win the conference, or even to win the national championship, there are always specific and identifiable roadblocks you will need to overcome.

Terry Pettit, former Nebraska volleyball coach, took this approach when he was targeting the national championship. He knew his team would run into Stanford in the NCAA tournament bracket, and he identified Kerri Walsh as the player his team would need to neutralize to defeat the Cardinal. He knew his team had a good block and he felt they could slow her down when she hit from the front row. However, he worried they would not be able to defend against Walsh when she hit from the back row, as it was not an attack they had seen from someone so capable.

To prepare for this one key player on the Stanford team, Pettit placed a hard-hitting male practice player, standing on a box, in the right-side back row position to hit against Nebraska's defense at the end of every practice. This enabled his team to work on the power and the angles he knew Walsh could hit.

Though his team eventually lost to Stanford, Pettit said:

"We wouldn't have won the first set if we didn't train for that situation all year long."

A fellow coach asked Pettit's advice after winning their first and second round matches in the NCAA tournament. They were preparing to meet an opponent in the Sweet 16 who was led by one of the best players in the nation. This player attacked the ball from extremely sharp angles, and the coach asked Pettit how to prepare for the star. Pettit replied:

"It's too late."

PROGRAMS DESIGNED TO WIN STILL HAVE LOW POINTS

Even teams that are designed to win will have low points. For Utah in 2019, the low point came in back-to-back victories over Arizona and Arizona State at home. It may seem odd that the low point came during a weekend with two conference wins. If you were simply competing hard, you would take the wins and be happy about them. But if you are designed to win, not everything is measured by wins and losses.

Utah had played well in the away matches against these two schools earlier in the conference schedule and had beaten Arizona 3-1 and Arizona State 3-0. The Arizona State match was a particularly strong performance, given key injuries to the starting setter and opposite hitter. The team had to rely on a first-year setter who had seen limited playing time and on an opposite with similarly limited experience. The bench stepped up and contributed to true team wins.

But it was a different story in the home matches versus Arizona and Arizona State later in the season. Utah looked tired, and the brutal Pac-12 season seemed to be wearing on them. They won both of the matches 3-2, but nothing was sharp. They had stopped communicating on the court, and it felt as if they had hit a wall.

In the locker room after the matches, the players were surprised to be held for a forty-five-minute difficult conversation with the coaches and, ultimately, with each other. In general, the players were happy to have two wins for the weekend and didn't see much of a problem. The coaching staff had to point out the lack of communication and the fact that if they didn't wake up, the rest of the season was going to be a challenge. They told the players, "You think everything is OK, but it is not. We have to start communicating more with each other. You can't just go through the motions and expect to be great." The team needed to find their passion again.

After the locker room talk, the coaches gave the players two days off to refresh themselves and reset their thinking. After the rest, the team got back on track and extended their winning streak to five matches. If you are designed to win, you can't be satisfied with just winning.

Patti Tibaldi, NAIA women's basketball Hall of Fame, said it well:

> "The instant one accepts mediocre play while still winning, whether that be by players or staff, it erodes the entire concept of being designed to win. Once you develop a culture that looks to achieve at the highest level, there is an understanding that less than that attitude is not acceptable."

RED-TAILED HAWKS VS. FIELD MICE

After six years in the Pac-12, Utah had renewed its program and all of the pieces were in place to win. But the team felt lost. The talent was there, the coaching was there, and the support was there. What wasn't there yet was a deep-seated belief that they truly deserved to be at the top of the conference.

Russ Franklin, 19-year Utah volleyball fan, gave this anecdote:

> "I once was told by a former assistant coach the week before an important road trip that 'I will be happy if we split this weekend' when I thought we should come home with a sweep."

The big challenge in dealing with this was that there wasn't a clearly identifiable problem to solve. As Beth put it at the time:

> "We had been so focused on building the program and chasing other teams, we just didn't know how to act when we were one of the better teams in the conference. It was easy and motivating while we were pursuing, but now it is getting hard as teams know we are good and we are the ones being pursued. We don't know how to handle it. I think the 'hard' is overtaking our drive. I think we are a little shaky on a clear objective. The team has goals, but to be honest, the way we have been playing lately, it is clear the team is not focused and we need to do something different. Direct and to the point is what we need right now. Everything had been all giggles when we were winning and now that teams are pursuing us, we're losing. We all know it's serious, and we are struggling with how to deal with it."

By this point, Beth and Leo had been working together for a couple of years. Beth wanted a different perspective, and she asked Leo to come up with something that would help the team see things in a new light. Creative leadership is called for in times such as these.

Leo believed that Utah's difficult experiences early on in the Pac-12 had imprinted on the minds of the staff and players. When Utah entered the Pac-12, they would go into matches hoping to win. As the program improved, the mindset then switched to competing to win. The thinking was that they were now good enough that they had a chance to win every match.

But that is not the mindset of the traditional national powers. These teams don't go into a match thinking that if they compete hard they will have a good chance at winning. They go into the match expecting to win. They are the predators, and their opponents are the prey. This became the main theme of Leo's talk with the team.

The talk began by thinking back to how Utah felt early on in the Pac-12 years. The Utes were field mice, scurrying around and hiding behind rocks to protect themselves from the predators surrounding them. Their goal was not to win but to survive.

But even though Utah had greatly improved its program and was clearly no longer the prey, that mindset remained. When you looked into the players' eyes during a tense match, you didn't see confidence. You saw FUD: Fear, Uncertainty, and Doubt. The players had the talent and training to win, but they were still hoping to win, not expecting to win.

Leo asked the team if they thought the traditional powers (Stanford, Nebraska, Penn State...) were afraid of playing Utah. They answered "No." When asked why, the players said that, rightly or wrongly, those teams expected to win. He then asked, "How do you qualify to be in the select club that goes into every match expecting to win?" The players were stumped and didn't have any good answers.

Leo then told them that no one will ever ask you to join this club. The only way to gain membership is to flip the switch in your mind and decide that you belong. Once you do that, you become the predator and the other teams become your prey. Late in the match when things get tough, it should be they that are fearing you, not the other way around. Utah needed to believe they were the red-tailed hawk (the University of Utah's mascot) that feeds upon the field mice.

The players connected with this. They realized that all they needed to do was to expect to win, and that the winning mindset was entirely under their control. One of the players in the session commented, "I never knew we could just decide on our own that we deserved to win."

At the next match, a red-tailed hawk plush toy had its own seat on the Utah bench. The team went on a five-match winning spree. They now saw themselves as being at the top of the food chain and believed deep down that the other teams were the ones who should be afraid. With a renewed hunger to win, it was time to feast.

THE IMPORTANCE OF A GROWTH MINDSET

Malia Shoji, University of Utah volleyball associate head coach, said:

> "You need to be innovative and push the dial in all aspects of your program, even after you have experienced success."

There are two ways of approaching the development of talent. Those with growth mindsets believe people can be developed into better versions of themselves through taking on challenges and the risks that go with them. They are constantly pursuing mastery of skills and of themselves, and they must do so because the margin of victory can be very thin.

As an example, Karch Kiraly coached the USA women's volleyball team to victory in the 2014 FIVB Volleyball women's world championship but, in the final match against China, each side scored exactly the same number of total points. He told us:

> "The margins are thin. You need to have a ruthless and never-ending pursuit of mastery at both the team and individual levels."

Those having a fixed mindset believe you are defined by the talents and capabilities with which you were born and that failure signals that your potential is low. It is hard to build a program designed to win with a fixed mindset since so much of a coach's effort is spent developing and growing players and support staff members.

A particularly negative aspect of a fixed mindset is that it tends to make people certain they are right when, in fact, they are not. Their fixed mindset encourages them to jump to a conclusion and to then defend it so they are not proven wrong. Someone with a growth mindset, on the other hand, will be open to exploring the possibility of being wrong and therefore will have a better chance of correcting their mistakes.

HAVING IDEAS OTHERS DON'T GIVES YOU A LASTING EDGE

Ideas for growth can come from anywhere, but it is easy to ignore those from outside what is considered typical in your sport.

Had Beth just humored Leo and not refined and incorporated any of his ideas, she would still be a highly successful coach. But by actively engaging and searching for new ideas and tools, she gained an edge. And since she looked where others have not, her edge persists.

Can ideas from outside of coaching really be applicable to your program? As an example, Jay Lund, Chairman, President, and CEO of Andersen Corporation, describes what is needed in a leader of a winning organization in this way:

- Deep understanding of the business.
- Vision.
- Inspired leadership.
- Courage and resiliency.
- Data-driven with an ability to connect the dots.
- Conviction balanced with judgment, objectivity, and humility.
- Results-driven.

If we hadn't said that was a business example, it would be hard for anyone to tell that his words did not come from a coach. Perhaps the worlds of coaching and business are not so different after all.

MEASURING SUCCESS IN A PROGRAM DESIGNED TO WIN

Programs designed to win don't solely measure success by their win/loss record. They also measure success as a sum of all the individual and team improvement gains, attained goals, and garnered rewards (whether internal or external) that contribute to overall program success.

Utah enjoyed many program, individual, and academic records in 2019. They, in fact, did do many things the program had never done before, even without getting past the NCAA Sweet Sixteen, the level they were trying to exceed. These included:

- Program

  ○ Finished 3rd place solo in the Pac-12 for their best Pac-12 finish ever.

  ○ Made it to the Sweet Sixteen in the NCAA tournament for the second time in three years.

  ○ Beat the Southern California Schools (UCLA and USC) both home and away for the first time in program history.

  ○ Led the Pac-12 in kills, blocks, assists, and points.

- Individual

  ○ Beth Launiere named Pac-12 and AVCA West Region Coach of the Year.

  ○ Dani Drews had 643 kills to lead the Pac-12 and set the Utah single-season record.

  ○ Saige Ka'aha'aina-Torres had 1,518 assists to lead the Pac-12 and set the Utah single-season record.

  ○ Berkeley Oblad set the career program record for most sets played (514) and most matches played (134).

  ○ Bri Doehrmann set the program record for career digs (1,646) and was five shy of the record for digs in a season (493).

  ○ All-Conference honors for Dani Drews, Kenzie Koerber, and Zoe Weatherington (Pac-12 All-Freshman Team).

  ○ AVCA All-American honors for Dani Drews (First

Team), Berkeley Oblad and Kenzie Koerber (Second
Team), and Saige Ka'aha'aina-Torres (Honorable
Mention).

° Berkeley Oblad and Bri Doehrmann signed
professional contracts to play in Europe after they
graduated.

• Academics

° Set an all-time high GPA record of 3.64.

° The team earned a perfect single-year Academic
Progress Rate (APR) score for the seventh consecutive
year and a perfect multiyear score for a fourth straight
season. APR accounts for eligibility, retention, and
graduation of all student-athletes on scholarship
and provides a measure of each team's academic
performance.

° Ten players received academic honors on the Dean's
List or Honor Roll.

MAIN POINTS IN THIS CHAPTER

• It is easy for management demands to take time away
from coaching.

• A lasting vision statement anchors a program and lets
everyone know what the program values while pursuing
excellence.

• If you are designed to win and you work hard, success
will follow. Even so, you will still have low points through
which you must fight.

- You can choose whether you are a field mouse hiding from the predators or if you are the red-tailed hawk instilling fear into the hearts of your prey.
- A growth mindset is fundamental to being designed to win.
- Programs designed to win measure success in many ways.

CHAPTER 3: STARS AND "C" PERFORMERS

"I don't live in a world of C performers."

Tara VanDerveer (Stanford women's basketball coach)

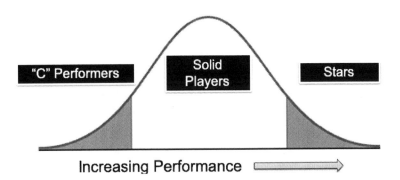

Figure 3-1: Defining stars and "C" performers

Setting and enforcing high expectations whose results can be measured and managed is fundamental to designing a program to win. If you are going to win at the highest level, your coaches, staff, and players must perform at that level. You must help your star performers realize their full potential, while also preventing your "C" performers from dragging everyone down.

Though we touch on solid players at the end of the chapter, we will primarily focus this chapter on the outliers—the stars who lift up your program and the "C's" who bring it down. As you read this chapter, you might wonder whether we are referring to your staff or your players. The answer is yes—the same ideas apply equally well to both groups.

When we talk about the downside of "C" performers in this book, we do so in the context of a program designed to win. Staff and players entering these programs have excelled in their previous roles and have made the cut to either be offered a job or a position on the team.

Contrast this with a high school program that takes in a much broader skill range of athletes. Even the lesser-skilled athletes benefit from playing sport at this level, and there may be many "C" players on the team. But the goals of these programs may be more about nurturing and developing young people and introducing them to a lifetime of teamwork and athletic activity than about winning at the highest level. As Patti Tibaldi, NAIA women's basketball Hall of Famer, told us:

"Sometimes, the athlete needs the sport more than the sport needs them."

CHARACTERISTICS OF A STAR

True stars are a rare treasure for your program and can make the difference between a good year and a great year. In fact, they can be program changers. But, just as stars in space warp space-time and cause the planets to orbit around them, your program's stars distort your world and cause ripples that are felt by all.

Stars possess an outsized influence in that they have huge roles on the court, gym pool, track, or field and are often leaders on your team. Among the benefits stars bring:

- Stars can carry your team on their backs when the game or match is on the line.
- They can challenge and inspire those around them to raise their performance beyond what they had thought possible.
- They bring greater attention to your program than what your win/loss record might normally attract. The media loves stars.
- They help your recruiting by showing the level of player your program can recruit, train, and produce, and by providing the opportunity for a young player to be a teammate of one of their idols.
- They can lead by example and show that even the most talented players benefit from putting in long hours of training and practice.

But stars also bring the possibility of distorting your program in negative ways. These include:

- Becoming overly reliant on your stars so that if they go down from injury, or if they occasionally struggle, there is little to back them up.
- Having teammates rely on them so much at the end of a contest that other players get complacent, knowing they probably will not be called upon to make the decisive play.
- Creating jealousy inside your team when those who train

hard but receive little recognition compare themselves to the stars and the praise lavished upon them by the fans and media. This jealousy is intensified if players believe (usually incorrectly) that the coach is pitching their stars to the media rather than talking about the team as a whole.

- Expecting to be treated by a different set of rules (or no rules at all) compared to the rest of the team.
- Becoming so irreplaceable that they still get playing time even when they lose interest and slack off. This sends a terrible motivational message to the rest of the team who crave playing time and are working hard to earn it.
- Creating conflicts with the coaching staff on what is best for the program vs. what is best for the star.

SETTING THE RIGHT GOALS FOR YOUR STARS

The challenge with star performers (both players and staff members) is that they can outperform others without having to work very hard to do so. Their sheer ability ensures they will virtually always beat average performers. The key is to set targets which are appropriate to the star's capability rather than setting the much lower targets that others may have to stretch to reach. What gets measured gets improved, and a star's goals need to be set high to unleash their full capabilities.

The targets for stars need to be set against their own already high level of performance or against outstanding players on other teams who have already reached the peaks your star is trying to climb. For example, if your star was a starter last season, what stats would they need to be named All-Conference? If they were

All-Conference, what stats would make them an honorable mention All-American? If they were an honorable mention All-American, what would it take for them to be named to the first or second All-American teams?

All of these numbers are easily identified by looking at the stats of players who have already reached your star's next goal. Present the numbers to your star, collaborate with them to set goals, and then step back and let them shine. Chances are they have a wonderful growth mindset based on their current success, and by challenging them they will stay focused on the next step in their development.

Setting targets is more difficult for your star staff members since they have few stats nor easily identifiable honors such as All-Conference or All-American. Instead, you will need to rely on your own evaluations of their skill levels. The targets you set with them will by necessity be focused primarily on internally perceived growth and development rather than on external validation.

With that said, you do have some external benchmarks you can use with your staff. If they are getting job offers from other programs, the coaching market is saying they are ready for the next step. You can monitor how their coaching network is growing to see how they are doing at building a presence in the profession. But at the end of the day, it is much harder to get external benchmarks for your staff than it is for your players.

DEVELOPING YOUR STARS TO THEIR FULL POTENTIAL

Stars need to be encouraged to develop, even when they are already better than their teammates. Dan Corotan, University of Utah volleyball assistant coach, said:

> "A star performer has a different mentality. I can push stars harder. They want that."

So, how do you develop your highest potential performers? Do the following:

- Let them know you see greatness inside them. Tell them you are committed to unleashing their potential to its fullest extent.
- Work with them to set challenging goals that are far beyond those of other individuals, but that are achievable by someone of their abilities.
- Let them know you care about them and that is why you will be pushing and challenging them.
- Provide guidance on how to continue to be a great learner even when they already win in practice every day.
- Don't compare them to others in your program. They are stars and they will outperform their teammates every day.
- Instill in them a sense of humility. When stars think of themselves as being better than other people, their growth slows and their attitude of entitlement and superiority may cause them to be a net negative for the team.

Jay Debertin, CEO of the Fortune 100 company CHS, believes stars need to be dealt with differently than average performers. There is always a best player on the team, and you need to rely on them when things are critical. He thinks most people understand this and can get their heads around why it is so.

But there is a limit, and it always comes down to people's basic sense of fairness. If the star is allowed to break the organization's rules and stop living by its values, people will begin to lose faith in the leader for tolerating it.

Stars need to be held to exactly the same cultural and behavioral standards as everyone else in the program, but they are not like the rest. When push comes to shove and the match is on the line, it is the stars who will make the difference between victory and defeat.

The late Mike Hebert, who Beth coached under at Illinois and who is an AVCA Hall of Famer, often said:

> "With one great player, you can be in the top half of your conference. With two great players, you will make a deep run in the NCAA championships. With three, you have a real shot at making the Final Four and contending for a national championship."

YOUR STARS MUST BE ENCOURAGED TO FAIL

If you are truly stretching your stars, they will fail at some point. As Green Bay Packers coach Vince Lombardi said, "If you are not making mistakes, you're not trying hard enough." Or, as racing legend Mario Andretti said, "If everything seems under control, you're just not going fast enough."

Your goal should not be to prevent your stars from failing to protect their fragile egos, but instead to push them so hard that they inevitably fail. When they do, you need to help them understand and accept that they failed, solidify what they learned from it, and then get them to dust themselves off and get back in the game.

The longer your best performers go without failing, the more they define their self-worth as being the person who never makes mistakes. Because of this, they will become more and more risk averse and will avoid doing anything that might not work out perfectly. This lowers their ceiling and downgrades a potential star into just a good performer. You only get so many potential stars, and you must do everything in your power to help them realize their full potential and maximize their value to your program.

CASE STUDY OF THE POWER OF FAILURE

Taylor Glenn was a reasonably accomplished juggler, and she started an Instagram channel where she posted a video of herself juggling every day for two straight years. But unlike most skilled people on the web, she didn't hide her failures. Whereas most people would shoot the same trick 50 times and only post the one attempt which made them look like they were true masters of a difficult skill, Glenn ended virtually all of her videos with one of her mistakes.

She would be doing a trick and the video would end with balls or clubs sailing out of the frame and hitting the floor. Glenn never failed on purpose. The videos showed her actual blunders as she was learning new tricks. When she got good enough at a trick not to fail, she moved on to the next trick and began failing once again.

Her channel began to pick up fans. First 1,000, then 10,000, and now 130,000. What fans comment on the most is her being totally unashamed of her failures. Everyone fails, but most people try to hide that fact or to minimize their failures by avoiding difficult things. But Glenn believes if she didn't push herself to fail, she wouldn't improve. She told us:

> "People think juggling is about throwing and catching objects. It is not. It is about throwing and dropping and throwing and dropping and throwing and dropping and then throwing and catching objects."

Here is the Guinness Book page highlighting the world record Glenn recently set for successfully performing 39 different three-ball juggling tricks in one minute:

Figure 3-2: Taylor Glenn, Guinness Book of World Records Holder

CASE STUDY OF A STAR

Kim Turner is one of the most decorated players in Utah volleyball history. She played for the Utes in the early 2000s and was instrumental in leading the team to its first-ever Sweet 16 in 2001. Turner was a four-time member of the Mountain West Conference (MWC) All-Conference team, a two-time MWC Player of the Year, and Utah's first AVCA All-American. She has been inducted into the Utah Crimson Club Hall of Fame and recently became the first Utah volleyball player to have her jersey retired— it now hangs in the rafters of the Jon M. Huntsman Center, alongside such basketball greats as Andre Miller, Andrew Bogut, and former coach Rick Majerus.

Other coaches may not have realized Turner's potential since she had not been highly recruited and had been overlooked by many top programs. But even in her first year, she took full responsibility as a leader of the team and never looked back. Turner was treated differently in that she was asked to carry so much of the program right away and throughout her career. She had an uncanny ability to absorb information and handle it with confidence and calm. The more she showed she could handle, the more leadership responsibility Turner was given. Every person on the court, on the bench, and in the stands knew Turner was both the best player and the team leader.

WHY YOU SHOULDN'T TREAT YOUR STARS LIKE FAMILY

While you may run your program with principles reflecting family values, you are not your team's parent. You are much closer to being the CEO of your program. You are being paid to achieve and win, and you must do everything you can within the boundaries of the rules and your overall vision to do so.

Programs that are simply competing hard spend much of their time dealing with the problems created by poor performers. Since stars usually don't create huge problems, coaches will tend to spend less time with those possessing the highest potential.

If your program really was a family, this would be exactly the right thing to do. After all, what would you do if you had a child who started acting up and getting into trouble? You wouldn't just give up on that kid and move on to the next one—no matter how much you might like to do so! Instead, you would spend more time and attention figuring out why they are acting up and how you could help them.

The challenge is that if you do the same in your program, you will doom it to mediocrity. Rather than pushing your stars to their fullest potential, you will spend all of your time with the lower-level performers trying to bring them up to a minimally acceptable level. Raising an end-of-the-bench player to the level of a second backup will not revolutionize your program, but helping one of your stars make All-American instead of simply All-Conference will do so.

Even if you wish it were not the case, coaching at some levels is a business. There is a great deal of money backing your program, and that backing comes with expectations of victory. This does not mean you do not care about players and staff in your program. In fact, it is through pushing your staff and players to their fullest potential that you show how strongly you care about them.

One other point on treating your team like a family. Families tend to be quite dysfunctional at times. You don't want "family" drama taking over your program. You are a professional and need to keep the focus on helping your team, not on trying and failing to keep everyone happy all the time.

THE TRUE COST OF A "C" PERFORMER IS FAR HIGHER THAN YOU THINK

When we refer to "C" performers, we are thinking of at most

5–10% of your coaching staff or players. "C" performers stand out from the pack, and not in good ways. The true cost of a "C" performer is much higher than you think.

Obviously, "C" performers do their own work much less effectively than either stars or solid performers. Their assignments come back late, unfinished, off target, or not to the level of quality required. Even though they don't deliver high-quality work, they often make the biggest demands on your time. They may want endless meetings to show you how clever they have been, or they might avoid you entirely and plan on surprising you with the brilliance of their work after it has been completed. Either way, they will not complete the task in the way you need it and will take more of your time than you had allotted.

If it was just the fact that they do their own jobs poorly, you might think it better to just ignore "C" performers and work around them. After all, you have many things to do and it takes time to deal with the issues "C" performers create. But if you want to design your program to win, you cannot let "C" performers hang on because they hurt your program in many more ways than just their own poor performance. Other ways they hurt your program include:

- "C's" block the advancement of more talented people. They don't deserve to be promoted, and no one else is clamoring to take them off of your hands. So, they clog up their spot and prevent you from using it to develop a potential star or solid performer.

- "C's" overload your top performers as they scramble to do the work that should have been completed by the "C's." This builds resentment amongst those who are actually doing the work and creates rifts within your program. Colorado State's volleyball coach, Tom Hilbert, told us of an assistant who underperformed in two of the three areas to which they were assigned. The players didn't know this since they don't see much of the work environment, but it caused resentment amongst the other staff members who were working hard on their own jobs and who also had to cover for the underperformer.

- "C's" create bottlenecks in projects that require inputs from multiple people. If the "C" does not deliver on time and to the level of quality required, they may impose delays on others who are dependent on the "C's" work to proceed.

- "C's" are poor role models and teachers for those below them. Therefore, the next generation develops more slowly—or not at all.

- "C" performers hire and promote other "C" performers. They will never bring stars into the program because they are afraid of being outshone.

Continued acceptance of "C" performance signals that either the leaders are clueless or they have lowered the bar. If you don't take action, you are signaling that the results being delivered by your "C" are perfectly acceptable to you.

The final point is that misery loves company. "C's" tend to be dissatisfied and generators of drama, gossip, and grievances. There is no way a program can be designed to win unless it sets and maintains high standards for everyone in the program, including the "C" players.

"C'S" THINK THEY ARE STARS

One of the biggest challenges of "C" performers is that they don't see themselves as they are. When "C's" look in the mirror, they see misunderstood stars who are constantly picked on and treated unfairly. They believe their lack of results and the negative feedback they receive has nothing to do with them and everything to do with those who are out to get them. This blocks them from working hard because they feel they already deserve more respect and playing time than they are getting. If they are being treated so unfairly, why work even harder?

John Dunning has coached his teams to five volleyball national championships. He emphasized the importance of bringing the "C" performer's underperformance out in the open. He told us:

> "You might think they are 'C's, but they think they are 'A's. You can't harshly evaluate people unless you've discussed it."

As part of the discussion, Dunning made sure to communicate to them what "A" performance looks like so they could visualize the targets he wanted them to meet. If the light turned on for them after this direct feedback, it signaled that they were able to learn and could still be developed. If it didn't, he had given them fair warning.

THE DIFFERENT CAUSES OF "C" PERFORMANCE

There are some behavioral characteristics that will turn anyone into a "C" performer. These include sexual harassment, racism, sexism, and any other behaviors that demonstrate a lack of respect for the dignity of others. If you can't counsel these behaviors out of someone, it is hard to see how they could fit in a program designed to win.

There are several other underlying causes of "C" performance. These include:

- Lack of experience. It may be the person has potential, but just doesn't have the experience yet to accomplish the work required of their role.

- Lack of talent. Some people just don't have the capability to do the job at the level required, no matter how much others try to help them. They may be wonderful team players, and you may greatly respect their effort, but not everyone has the raw ability to fill the roles you need.

- Lack of effort or motivation. Athletics is a demanding field, and it requires a commitment of time and energy. If someone does not want to commit at that level or is unable to do so, it is unlikely they will contribute to a winning program.

- Lack of discipline and mental toughness. Some people have the capability to excel but get off track when things don't work out as they had hoped or as quickly as they would have liked. They need to thrive on competition, not wilt from it.

- Lack of confidence. They may be able to do the work, but simply not have confidence in their own abilities. If that is the case, they will become tentative and will be slow to build the string of successes that would increase their confidence level.

- Lack of understanding of their sport. Many people

are unwilling to dive into the details in the way that is required to develop a deep understanding of their sport and what it takes to succeed in it. If you don't have relevant content knowledge, it's hard to pass it on to others.

- Poor interpersonal skills. Some people have the ability to contribute, but their personality and weak interpersonal skills don't allow them to work well with others.

- Poor communication and behavioral skills. Everyone has their own preferred communication and behavioral styles. Not everyone in your program needs to have the same style, but the strengths and weaknesses of each person should be known and appreciated.

- Lack of understanding or acceptance of their role. Occasionally, someone will see their role as being much grander than the one they are actually expected to fill. This can lead to them overstepping the boundaries of their position and making moves that are not consistent with the vision of the program. Beth had this experience with a staff member who felt they could take the program where they saw fit, as opposed to executing the plan Beth had already chosen.

- Distractions with other priorities in their lives. It may be that the cause of poor performance is temporary. Demands on their time from family, friends, and other interests may be acceptable if they happen for short periods of time. But if these demands persist and don't appear likely to ever go away, the individual may not be a good fit in the exacting world of athletics.

- Not understanding why they are part of the program. Tom Farden, Utah gymnastics coach, told us that in his sport the "C" performers are the athletes that could never answer the "Why?". Why are they a part of the program? Why did they engage during the recruiting process, and why are they still in the sport? Without understanding their "Why?", they are not dedicated enough to win each repetition or to compete every day to beat others out for a starting job.

- Mismatch between assignments and capabilities. Some people may be stars in some areas and "C's" in others. If so, they may still be able to contribute to your program if you focus their assignments on their strengths and avoid their weaknesses.

IT TAKES A LOT OF WORK TO BE A "C" PERFORMER

Many "C" performers retain their roles because they learn to game the system. Being this type of a "C" performer requires a lot of hard work. Or rather, it takes a lot of effort to hide the fact that they aren't doing any work.

The most common approach to covering for a lack of effort and results is to flatter and be attentive to your boss, and to ignore or even be abusive to those below you. In business, this is called "Kiss up, kick down." In academics, it is sometimes called "Shine and slime." Shine up, slime down.

This approach is a form of gaslighting in which those below the "C" begin to question their own reality. Every day, they see the actual performance of the "C" and the ripple effect it has on the rest of the organization. But when they hear the boss talk about the person, they do so in glowing terms. Often, the boss is being served well by the "C," since that is where all the "C's" effort goes. The boss sees competence, while those below see someone incapable of doing their job, and they wonder how the boss could be so clueless as to not see what is self-evident.

"C" performers are also masters at dodging accountability. When asked to take on a task or a project, they will say yes, giving all the signals of being a solid team player. Then, they simply will not do the work. If asked, they will say the work is in progress. They will never go on the record refusing a task or project. They will just smile, say "got it, Boss!" and then forget about it before they leave the room, or simply make a conscience choice to not do the job.

If "C" performers focused the effort they spend on avoiding work on actually doing work, they would instantly transform into high "B's."

HOW YOU MIGHT BE ENABLING "C" PERFORMERS

Sometimes, the "C" performer doesn't bear all the responsibility for poor performance. You may be enabling their performance by the way you work with them.

First, you may be creating a self-fulfilling prophecy. If you believe someone to be a "C" performer and send signals in every interaction that that is the case, they will perform down to what they perceive you expect of them.

Second, you might be unclear or incomplete in your requests, so they start out not fully understanding what you need from them. Because they didn't understand what you wanted in the first place, it is highly unlikely they will come back with something that wows you.

Third, you may be setting them up to fail by delegating tasks or projects they are not yet capable of successfully completing. If you delegate something that should have been given to someone with more experience, you may doom the effort to failure from the outset. You want to stretch your people, but not break them with impossible assignments.

Fourth, you may send both verbal and non-verbal signals to a struggling staff member or player that you have lost confidence in them. One of the most common signals is to avoid eye contact with them. The underperformer will pick up on this and begin to feel isolated. They will lose confidence and begin to feel like they are not a valued member of the team.

Rather than enabling "C" performers, you could go in the other direction and develop a mentality that simply does not accept a subpar level of performance. If you do so, you will need to increase your training, systems, and knowledge base to give everyone the tools required for improving their performance. After you have given everyone a fair chance, however, you could simply make the deliberate choice to remove "C" performers from your world.

RECOGNIZING "C" PERFORMERS

If you have the feeling someone is a "C" performer, you are probably right. "C" performers send numerous signals that they are struggling in their roles. But given the time required to deal with them, it is tempting to ignore these signals. Just having one bad day does not qualify someone as being in this category, but a continuing pattern should make you stop and reassess their capabilities and fit.

On the other hand, you might think someone is a "C" performer, but you may be wrong. Always make sure you speak with the person and with others who work closely with them so that you have all the facts. Maybe they are just waiting for your guidance and encouragement. Perhaps they are actually delivering more than you give them credit for and they are not the issue you thought they were. If you were mistaken about them, own up to it and admit you were wrong.

Beth has been in this situation, and it is easy to misunderstand what has actually been happening. Often a staff member has done the work but has not shown it to her. Or they were working on a long-term project and haven't kept her informed of their progress. Or perhaps they quickly finished a task but didn't report to Beth that they had completed it. These problems might cause someone to appear to be a "C" performer when the fact is they are simply not communicating effectively. When Beth has been in this situation, she has been pleasantly surprised when the facts were brought to her attention.

People who are new in their job deserve the benefit of the doubt because they are still learning their roles. You brought them into the program for a reason, and you should not give up on them immediately. They may grow into their role as they gain experience and confidence.

With that said, the vast majority of coaches will say they wish they had acted sooner than they did to deal with a "C" performer. Almost none have said they acted too quickly and that things would have gotten better if only they had waited.

People may be stars in some areas and "C's" in others. If so, they may still be able to contribute to your program if you focus their efforts on their strengths and avoid their weaknesses. This comes with a caveat that doing so may help the program but may stall their personal development since it allows them to avoid improving on their areas of weakness.

Finally, the more experience you have, the harder it may be for you to remember how difficult it was when you first started. It is a common error to assume that something that seems simple to you could be easily handled by someone with a tiny fraction of your experience. If you don't make allowances for the experience gap, you may evaluate people too harshly and write them off before they have a chance to prove themselves.

THOUGHTS ON "C" PERFORMERS FROM A FORTUNE 100 CEO

Jay Debertin, CEO of CHS, had insightful thoughts on "C" performers. Many team members take their failure personally. That is understandable, but normally, the issue is not ability, but the wrong fit. When Debertin deals with a "C" performer, he is empathetic and tells them:

> "I put you in the wrong spot and this is not going to work. You are not going to go home to your family and feel fulfilled."

The issue can be even worse when the "C" performer is a leader in the organization. "A" and "B" performers will be frustrated working under a "C," and will quickly leave for better opportunities in a different organization. Once the top performers have left, all that remains is a hollow organization and an underperforming team. Debertin summarized his view with this quote:

> "A" players hire "A" players.

"B" players hire "C" players.

"A" players won't work for "C" players.

"C" players won't last long working for "A" players.

DEALING WITH "C" PERFORMERS

The most common path to dealing with "C" performers is to work around them and hope that things somehow improve on their own. The reasoning behind this approach is that it would take a lot of time to improve their performance and you won't get much return on the time you would have to invest to make it happen. If you follow this approach, however, you will be dragging out your problems rather than fixing them.

As Greg Cygan, president of Heritage Oak Private School and volleyball club director, told us:

> "In a private school, "C" performers glow like a 250W bulb in the dead of night. The parents know it, the other teachers know it, and the students know it. You need to be very, very clear with the expectations, match them up with a mentor, and quickly determine how long they will be allowed to stay in your organization. Once you have concluded that they are not willing, or not able, to make the necessary adjustments, you have to let them go. The faster the better. I find that I am much faster in wanting to change out an ineffective teacher. On some occasions, patience is rewarded. In most cases, it isn't."

The first step with a "C" performer is to sit down with them and give them accurate and honest feedback. Now is not the time to smooth things over. You owe them the harsh truth so that they have a chance to improve. If you are straight with them and they don't improve, the fault is theirs. If you do not give them the hard feedback they need, the fault rests on your shoulders. Don't wait until the right moment to give them feedback. They need to know as soon as you see serious deficiencies, and the right moment may never come.

Sometimes "C" performers are in a different department and not under your direct control. Examples of this would include your strength and conditioning coaches, trainers, compliance, marketing, etc. Even if they do not report to you, you have to rely on their assistance to win. The key is to set expectations for them at the same level you set for the people who work directly under you. If those in other departments don't meet your expectations, you will need to speak with their boss and address the issues.

If you need to go over their heads, you are not doing so to complain. You are simply stating the requirements of your plan to win. If they want to make the case that winning is not that important, let them. That will be a hard case to make, and it will be laughed at by your athletic director. As long as your focus is on your plan to win, and you are not asking people outside of your department to do more than you ask of those within your department, your focus on winning will be difficult to argue against.

John Dunning, former Stanford volleyball coach, emphasized that the style he used in these difficult conversations was matter-of-fact and non-emotional. He wasn't pointing out their failures as human beings, he was giving them honest and clear feedback so they knew where they stood and how they were progressing. He performed regular evaluations with both coaches and players with the one distinction being that "coaches don't have stats."

He believes you can't harshly evaluate people unless you have discussed the issues with them. Not only is it important to let them know why their performance level is unacceptable, you also need to communicate to them what an "A" or a star performance level looks like. They need to understand where the bar is set, not just that they are not clearing it. He told us:

> "You need to evaluate, plan, then reevaluate. If it is not working out, you are enabling them by keeping them in the program and it may be time to cut bait."

Patti Tibaldi, NAIA women's basketball Hall of Famer, uses a three-part test to evaluate whether someone who is currently a "C" performer has a chance to improve. The three parts are:

- **Do they get it?** Do they understand that their performance is not acceptable and that they are in danger of losing their position if they don't make significant improvements?
- **Do they go after it?** Are they facing the hard truths and committing their full effort to turning themselves around and becoming a positive contributor to your program?
- **Do they have the capability to change and grow?** They may be fully committed and trying to improve, but they may not have the capability to do so.

If the answer to any of these three questions is a clear "No," it is unlikely the "C" performer will ever improve beyond their current level.

TOOL: THE LEFT-HAND COLUMN

The "Left-Hand Column" tool, popularized by Peter Senge in his book *The Fifth Discipline,* helps you deal with difficult conversations. To use the tool, begin by drawing a vertical line to create two columns. In the right-hand column, put the things you were going to say that are toned down. Things like "I would like to see you spend more time on this." Or, "Could you up the urgency a bit?" Someone could hear these words and think they are minor suggestions, but that everything is basically OK.

In the left-hand column, you list the hard truths. Things such as "You let the team down on your last three assignments." Or "I can give you until the end of the season, and if you haven't radically improved, I am going to let you go."

If you started with the left-hand column, it would be too direct. The person would look for excuses as to why you are wrong rather than incorporating your honest feedback. To avoid this, start by quickly going through the right-hand column and then say, "This is what I had planned on saying. But if I am honest with myself and with you, this is what I really think." Then walk them through the left-hand column.

By hearing the softer points in the right-hand column first, the person opens a bit to feedback. Then when you go through the left-hand column, you are treating the person with respect. You are hard on the performance, but sensitive on the person.

DEALING WITH YOUR "B'S", THE SOLID PERFORMERS

The vast majority of people are solid performers who are neither stars nor "C's." They contribute to the program at about the level expected, and their roles are critically important to the success of your team. You can't ride them every day on the same thing, but it is your job to help them reach as high a level as their talent and effort allows.

You will never have a team entirely composed of stars, and if you ever did, the difficulty of managing expectations and deciding on playing time might make you regret that you wished for it. Your solid performers' roles are just as important to your team's success as that of your stars. It is true that a "B" won't be able to put the program on their back in the way a star could, but they can and should take pride in bringing value to the team from their seat on the bus.

Your solid performers need to understand their roles, and they need to be developed to strengthen your team. And since the solid performers make up the bulk of your team, they are the ones who bring the diversity that strengthens your program.

YOUR SOLID PERFORMERS AS THE "OTHERSIDE"

Jill Hirschinger, former UNH volleyball coach, told us:

> "Teams are only as good as their 3rd outside hitter or their 3rd middle blocker."

The third players on the depth chart will not see significant playing time in competitive matches. But that does not mean their role lacks value. What it means is that much of their contribution is delivered outside the bright lights of the arena or playing field. One of their critical jobs is to push the starters hard enough during practice that they continue to develop. Hirschinger refers to the solid performers as the "otherside."

If the "otherside" can't push the stars and the rest of the starters, there will be a limit on how much of the stars' and starters' potential will be developed. The starters will win most drills and scrimmages during practice. But if they can coast to a victory over the "otherside," it will be much harder for the starters to stay engaged and to push themselves.

But if the "otherside" can sometimes strike fear into the starters, and occasionally give them a wake-up call by beating them in a drill, the growth of your top players will continue and will reach a higher level.

Coaches can also split up their best players to raise the level of competition. Stars need to go against stars a certain percentage of the time in practice. In many women's sports, male practice players are added to bring size and strength to the "otherside."

The next time your team jumps in the air and runs to the net to celebrate their victory over a tough conference or playoff opponent, remember that much of the credit should go to the players on the end of the bench. Fans see them cheering their teammates on but may not understand that they contributed to the win even though they never got into the match.

Coaches, on the other hand, must appreciate their solid players' critical role in the development of the team that was on the court during crunch time. You will never go wrong by giving your "otherside" the thanks and congratulations due them for their role in preparing your starters for victory.

Mary Wise, Florida volleyball coach, highlighted an issue for performers at all levels. She sees a gap between what the coaches expect from a player and the player's own expectations. In her mind, this disconnect causes the most stress for coaches. She says:

> "So much of my job is to help her expect more out
> of herself. We aren't going to lower the program's
> standards to meet her, so time and effort has to be

spent teaching the player to raise her standards to the level the team requires."

MAIN POINTS IN THIS CHAPTER

- Stars can impact your program in both positive and negative ways.
- You must push your stars to their full potential. Occasional failures are a necessary part of the process of doing so.
- The true cost of a "C" performer is far higher than you think.
- Though it is always easier to let a "C" player or staff member slide, programs that are designed to win deal with their "C's."
- The Left-Hand Column tool helps you hold difficult conversations that address the real issues.
- You must set high expectations for everyone, tailored to their individual strengths, weaknesses, and capabilities.

CHAPTER 4: THE POWER OF DELEGATION

"If maybe I gave attention to everything, I might do it better…
but I wouldn't because I wouldn't have enough time."

Terry Pettit (former Nebraska volleyball coach)

Effective delegation is the cornerstone of leading and managing your program. Delegation ensures that the right work gets done by the right people, and it frees up higher-level leaders to do the work only they can do.

THE GOLDEN RULE OF DELEGATION

There is a golden rule that simplifies and clarifies decisions as to what to delegate. The golden rule is this:

Anything that **can** be delegated **must** be delegated.

It is this single statement that started Beth on her journey with

Leo. He mentioned it to her at a lunch, and it stuck in the back of her mind. Beth kept trying to understand how she could apply this and what the implications would be should she adopt the golden rule. Her acceptance of this rule was their first big step in working together.

Without the golden rule, delegation is a complicated process. You must first decide if a task or project should be delegated. To do that, you will need to balance priorities, capabilities, workloads, trust, and urgency. Then, for each of the things you have chosen to delegate, you need to decide to whom you will delegate it and then actually delegate it and ensure the person understands exactly what you need.

But you only need to decide one time to accept the golden rule, and once you do, your life is simplified. You will no longer need to spend a lot of time and energy deciding whether or not to delegate each task or project. Instead, all you need to ask yourself is if there is anyone below you in the organization who could credibly perform the work. If there is, you delegate to them. It is that simple.

Tara VanDerveer, Stanford women's basketball coach, believes that effective delegation was natural when we were children, but we have forgotten about it along the way. She said:

> "My parents delegated chores and they had it down to a science. Dad would show me how to do it the first time, and then I was expected to do it myself and you just got it done. Mom even had a saying for it - everyone works and no one works too hard."

YOU CAN'T SAY "YES!" UNTIL YOU LEARN TO SAY "NO."

Delegation is essentially the art of saying "No" to doing work yourself that could be done by someone who reports to you. You cannot master delegation until you master the art of saying "No" respectfully and with finality. Mahatma Gandhi summarized the importance of saying "No" when he said:

> "A 'No' uttered from deepest conviction is better and greater than a 'Yes' merely uttered to please, or what is worse, to avoid trouble."

As William Ury points out in his book *The Power of a Positive No*, you can't enthusiastically say "Yes!" to high-value tasks unless you free up your time by saying "No." to lower-value tasks. In other words, you say "No." with a period so you can say "Yes!" with an exclamation point.

If you do a small number of important things, you can do them with excellence and bring great value to your program. If you try to do a large number of important and unimportant things all mixed together, you will get little done and add little value. As Warren Buffett, CEO of Berkshire Hathaway, says:

> "The difference between successful people and really successful people is that really successful people say no to almost everything."

Saying "No." requires balancing your power and your relationships. If you exercise your power to say "No." too often, you could damage your relationships. People may become offended because they wanted you to agree to do the work they had requested.

But if you always say "Yes," it takes away your ability to control your own life and work. It also reduces the respect others have for you. Someone who always says "Yes" signals they have no higher priorities and are not focusing on the small number of things that matter.

There is also a sense of satisfaction that arises from a strong and confident "No." As Elizabeth M. Thackeray, MD, University of Utah Anesthesiology Residency Program Director, told us:

> "I was surprised at how empowering it felt to say "No." I felt a surge of confidence: I was taking control over my time and my attention, which are my most valuable (and nonrenewable) resources. My "No." defined my priorities and I refused to allow anyone else to define them for me. It felt fantastic!"

About 3 years ago, Beth began to say "No." to committee work for the American Volleyball Coaches Association (AVCA). She felt it was time for younger coaches to take over leadership roles in the organization, and she reached out to them to encourage their involvement. Slowly, younger coaches began taking over the responsibilities of building the sport.

By saying "No." to committee work, Beth has been able to say "Yes!" to writing this book, doing special projects for the AVCA, coaching more USA national teams, and getting involved in other coaching organizations such as WeCoach, Art of Coaching, and Gold Medal Squared.

Here is a great way of deciding whether or not to accept a project or task:

> "If it is not a 'Hell Yeah!', it's a 'No.'"

PEOPLE JUDGE YOUR VALUE BASED ON WHAT THEY SEE YOU DO

Just as effective delegation requires learning to say "No.", it also requires learning to prioritize your work based on the value it adds. You get paid the same amount every day, but you don't add the same amount of value every day. Depending on what work you choose to take on in a given day, you may create enormous value or only a negligible amount.

How you are perceived is based on the work people see you do. When people see you doing high-value work, they see you as being worth more than you are being paid, and so they recognize your benefit to the program. When they see you doing low-value work, they will begin to wonder about your capabilities. They will be surprised because they thought you were beyond that in your career.

For example, when you are making photocopies, the value you are adding to your program is $12 an hour, since that is what you would pay someone to make copies. Similarly, as a head coach, you will never impress your athletic director by doing your assistant coaches' jobs better and faster than they can.

Leo learned firsthand how people's perceptions of your value change when they observe you doing low-value tasks. He had developed a strong relationship with his biggest client from the previous two years, and it appeared he would provide services to them for many years to come. But then he was asked by one of the senior executives to sit in on a series of meetings with the CEO and the leadership team on a particularly sensitive decision. The executive did not want Leo to run the sessions, just to be in the room and be ready to intervene in case the discussion went off the rails.

Leo attended four of these meetings, and after that, he was never hired by the client again. Even though the CEO and the leadership team members all had personal experience working with Leo on high-value projects, when they saw him sitting on the side of the room doing nothing, their view of him changed. When they had seen Leo leading challenging sessions, they viewed him as being worth more than he cost. When they saw him sitting passively in a meeting and contributing nothing, they downgraded their view and stopped thinking of him as someone who added value.

THE VALUE YOU ADD DEPENDS ON THE WORK YOU CHOOSE TO DO

The golden rule tells you to delegate everything you can, but it doesn't tell you what to do with the time you free up. Choosing what work to retain requires prioritization and an analysis of high- and low-value uses of your time.

Think back on all of the ways you spent your time in the past year. Then ask yourself this question—what percent of your time was spent on things that could have been delegated, turned out not to matter, or that shouldn't have been done in the first place? Typically, responses are in the range of 30–40% of people's time that was spent on work in these categories.

That is one to two days a week of your most precious commodity (time and attention) tied up on work that others could have accomplished nearly as well as you could have. And that means you missed the opportunity to spend two days a week doing the work that only you could do.

There is a tool that identifies high- and low-value uses of your time. It is called the leadership agenda.

TOOL: THE LEADERSHIP AGENDA

The leadership agenda tool divides your work into two types: above the line and below the line. Above-the-line activities are high-value uses of your time, while below the line are low-value topics.

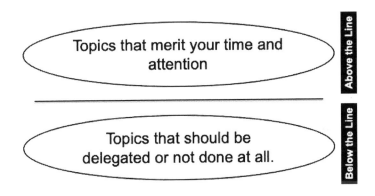

Figure 4-1: The leadership agenda tool

To create a leadership agenda, go to a wall or whiteboard and create a horizontal line with a marker or tape. Then, create a list of all the topics you could spend your time on in the coming months. Write each topic on a Post-it note, with one topic per note. Then go through them one at a time. If the topic is of high value and should be retained, place it above the horizontal line. If it is a lower-value topic that should be delegated or not done at all, place it below the line.

After you place each of the topics either above the line or below the line, do a second iteration. When you do your second pass you will realize some of the topics you placed above the line early on aren't really all that important when you compare them to the other above-the-line items.

When Beth did this for her program, she started by laying the topics out in great detail:

• Recruiting (working with assistants, evaluation, building relationships, campus visits, closing the deal.)
• Holding player meetings, teaching volleyball and life lessons through volleyball.
• Analyzing stats with coaching staff.
• Watching game video.
  – By self to analyze our team and the competition.
  – With players for their development and opponent scouting, and for a personal touch point with them.
• Marketing.
• Efficient brainstorming meetings.
	• Training and developing new assistants. Helping them transition from the informal world of club to the professional world of a university.
	• Maintaining strong working relationships with athletes, staff, and administration.
	• Education and support of the sport (clinics, legislative input, AVCA, national issues…)
	• Donor relations.
	• Trying for as much work/life balance as is possible given coaching demands.
	• Performance (strength coach, trainers, nutritionists, sports scientists…)
		Above the Line

• Sole designer of practice plans. • Double checking things that should have already been taken care of at a lower level. • Dealing with travel itineraries and other logistical details. • Schedules (players, marketing, academic…) • Managers and male practice players.	• Pointless meetings without purpose or accomplishments. • Administrative tasks (setting up player meetings, photocopying…) • Equipment. • Summer camp logistics. • Too involved with legwork of all aspects of the program.	**Below the Line**

Figure 4-2: Beth's initial leadership agenda

Her next step was to see if the topics could be grouped into a smaller number of categories. By looking for connections in the above-the-line items, Beth came up with the following:

• **Player development.** • **Team development.** • **Recruiting.**	**Above the Line**
• Things you do yourself that could have been delegated. • Things you delegated, but that require follow-up due to competency/trust issues. • Things that shouldn't be done at all.	**Below the Line**

Figure 4-3: Beth's leadership agenda with consolidated categories

This provided Beth with the clarity she had been seeking. When it comes down to it, there are only three high-value activities she should spend her time on. If a task is not connected to player development, team development, or recruiting, it should be delegated or not done at all.

In addition, there are only pieces of each of these three that merit a head coach's time. For example, in recruiting, it is a great use of Beth's time to close the deal with a recruit and their parents. However, there are many other activities within recruiting, including canvassing club tournaments looking for the initial talent pool, managing the database, making initial phone calls to club coaches, and arranging campus visits, that can and should be delegated.

When Beth started to work on her initial leadership agenda, she expressed a major concern: what if everything she did could be delegated and there was nothing left above the line? She needn't have worried. For a head coach, there will always be above-the-line items that merit time and attention, it's just a matter of identifying them. The reason you may not be aware of them is that so much of your time is currently taken up by below-the-line items. What Beth discovered was that by following the golden rule of delegation, she freed up time to unleash her creativity on the small number of things that truly matter at her level.

With all of this said, there are still occasional high-level compliance adherence, donor relations, academics, and marketing topics that require her attention. But the vast majority of a Beth's time is now spent on her three above-the-line topics.

DELEGATION CASCADES
THROUGH YOUR PROGRAM

Every coach has topics they should delegate to their workers and topics that have been delegated to them by their boss. This cascading nature of delegation looks like this:

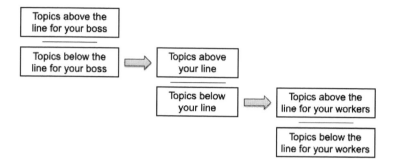

Figure 4-4: Delegation cascade with the leadership agenda.

This cascade was highlighted by Jamie Morrison, former head coach of the Dutch women's national volleyball team, when he told us:

> "Instead of thinking I had 50 hours to get things done in a week, I starting thinking that my staff of 5 people had 250 hours each week and it was my job to optimize that 250."

ABOVE-THE-LINE EXAMPLE: RECRUITING

An example of the power of prioritizing and freeing up time came when Beth was recruiting Adora Anae from Hawaii. Anae had not been heavily recruited when she committed to Utah, but as time went on, several other top-level coaches began to take notice of her. Beth deeply believed in Anae's potential and wanted to make sure she didn't lose her to another program. The best way to accomplish that was to visit her and her family in Hawaii.

But visiting Hawaii would not be easy since the season was already underway. Though desperate to take a break at the end of the preseason, Beth used the long weekend before the start of the conference grind to fly out to visit Anae and reconfirm her verbal commitment to Utah. Beth returned (after taking a vacation day, because come on!) to Utah comforted by the fact that any uncertainty about Anae coming to Utah had been removed.

Anae went on to a stellar career as a Ute. She became Utah's first-ever player to be named to the Pac-12 All-Freshman first team. She went on to become the first Ute to win back-to-back AVCA All-American awards and the first ever to win first-team honors. After graduating from Utah, Anae played professionally in South Korea where she led the league in scoring in her first year.

How much value did Beth add to Utah's program by making the trip to Hawaii to lock in Anae's commitment? The days she spent on this trip could easily have added 100 times as much value as she would have added on typical days.

The only reason Beth was able to make this trip during the season was because she had freed up her calendar by delegating all that could be delegated. Locking in Anae was something only the head coach could do and, as such, was an extremely high-value use of Beth's time.

THE SINGLE WORST APPROACH TO DELEGATION YOU CAN TAKE

There is a terrible approach to delegation that is difficult to resist. It is most people's first instinct, and it raises its ugly head again and again. The single worst approach you can take to delegation is this:

"I can do it better and faster myself."

Of course you can do it better and faster yourself. That is why you were promoted. But the question is not, "Can I do it better and faster myself?" The question is, "What value will be lost if I do work someone else could have done instead of doing the work that only I can do?"

The statement that you can do it better and faster yourself is almost assuredly correct. It will take longer to explain how to do the task and describe what you want than to do it yourself. That will be true every single time.

But tasks repeat. An individual task may take three times as long to delegate as it would take to just do it yourself. But if that task, or one similar to it, comes up 20 times later on, investing the time and training to delegate it will pay off in the long run.

When you delegate a task today, you are making an investment that will be repaid many times over by enabling you to confidently delegate that same category of task in the coming months and years. And, by doing so, you will be building the capabilities of your team, which will enable delegation of even more complex topics at a later date.

As Jamie Morrison, former head coach of the Dutch women's national volleyball team, told us:

> "Head coaches need to think of themselves as less of doers within their organizations and more as planners, organizers, and delegators."

WHAT IF THERE IS NO ONE TO WHOM YOU CAN DELEGATE?

If the first response to delegation is "I can do it better and faster myself," the second is "There is no one below me to whom I can delegate!"

Virtually all programs are lean, and no one has enough time to do all the work they have been allotted. Your natural tendency may be to ask for additional funding so you can hire more help. But your boss is just as overworked as you are, and you may be told to "Figure it out!" just as your boss must do.

It is true you are overworked. It's also true that you need more help. But saying so is unlikely to get you the help you need. A better approach is to go to your boss with a value story like this: "Boss, do we really want to pay someone $30 an hour to do a task that could have been done by someone making $12 an hour?"

When you ask for more people, that is seen as a cost to your organization. When you talk about offloading work to lower-paid people, that is seen as an investment that will produce a return.

If you can't get budgetary approval for additional workers, consider delegating some of your tasks to your players. They may be excited to handle activities such as posting on social media, designing T-shirts, creating videos to play on the scoreboard, creating playlists for pre-game warm-ups, etc.

There is another alternative, which is to simply not do the work at all. Just because you can think of a task or project and other people tend to do that type of work doesn't mean you have to do it. If it is a low-value topic, you are probably better off just leaving it below your line and not doing it rather than taking time away from higher-value topics.

HIRING LOWER-PAID WORKERS IS A GREAT INVESTMENT

Hiring lower-paid full- or part-time workers to free up the time of more experienced people is one of the best investments your program can make. One of Beth's former assistants, JJ Van Niel, was a master at this.

Van Niel is a high-level analytics expert, and he needs large amounts of data to do his work. At first Beth didn't understand why he was asking to hire people to assist him in gathering and entering data. Once she saw what Van Niel was able to do with the data, however, she understood the value of his approach and why he needed assistance.

Beth found money in the budget to hire people to enter data so that Van Niel could spend all of his time analyzing the data in ways only he could do. Because Van Niel was seen as a leader in applying data to athletics, finding workers was not a problem. He had eager young people who wanted to enter the field of data analytics lined up to work for him.

TRULY DELEGATING VS. KIND-OF DELEGATING

There is a simple and crystal-clear test to tell if you are truly delegating or just kind-of delegating. If you are truly delegating, the task comes off of your to-do list. If you are kind-of delegating, you do not have confidence it will be done to the quality level required by the time it is needed, so the task stays on your to-do list. You know you will have to circle back to make sure it actually gets done.

When you truly delegate, you empower your people and un-leash their creativity. This enables them to test their limits and re-alize their full potential. They will not simply follow your detailed instructions but will complete the work using their best judgement and ideas. They won't approach it exactly as you would have, but for 90% of topics, that is OK. For the other 10%, you will need to intervene and explain why you are doing so.

Tom Hilbert, Colorado State volleyball coach, said:

> "If you stifle an assistant from the beginning, they will be tentative when it comes to teaching. If you al-low them to teach on their own, the worst thing that can happen is you simply correct them, and both of you will learn from that."

Beth's Director of Operations Sheldon Carvalho experienced this firsthand when he was a volunteer assistant for her the year before. As the volunteer, he was normally second or third in line, and there were always more senior assistants with overlapping re-sponsibilities. His experience changed when Beth decided to give him full responsibility for training the liberos. His pride in the program grew, and he knew he had to step up his game because now he was in charge of something important. And the liberos benefitted from having a coach totally focused on their growth.

As Jill Hirschinger, UNH volleyball coach (and the person who gave Beth her first coaching job), put it:

> "The more you delegate, the more ownership some-one will take in the program."

Showing appreciation pays outsized benefits when you truly delegate. You are asking the person to take on work that will stretch them and will require effort. By showing your appreciation at the successful completion of the effort, you are setting things up for the next successful delegation. As John Dunning, American Volleyball Coaches Association Hall of Famer, said:

> "Share the credit. Let the people who do the work present it. Let them know you support what they are doing and let them be in charge of something in which they can take pride. And then show them the ultimate confidence by not worrying."

YOU CAN'T DELEGATE RESPONSIBILITY

Running an effective organization requires delegation. But doing so opens you up to taking the heat for someone not delivering for you. You can delegate tasks and projects, but you can't delegate responsibility.

When your people don't deliver, you must hold them accountable. You need to point out where they went off track and let them know what could have been done differently. You are not looking for excuses, you are looking to get the job done.

But just as you hold your people accountable, your boss will hold you accountable. It doesn't matter if you were the one who did the work or if you delegated it to someone else. It doesn't matter if there is an excuse for not delivering. What matters is that it was your responsibility to complete the work and it was not finished on time with the quality required. You are responsible, and there is no getting around it.

If you delegated the task to someone who was overloaded and couldn't do it in time, you are responsible. If the person didn't have the skills to complete the task, you are responsible. If they let the task slide and you didn't know about it, you are responsible. Welcome to being a leader.

WHY IS IT DIFFICULT TO TRULY DELEGATE?

Even when it is clear which topics should be delegated, it is still difficult to do so. Among the reasons for this are:

- It may not be clear to whom you should delegate each topic.
- You may not have sufficient trust and confidence in the people to whom you are delegating.
- The tendency to micromanage and be in control of everything is a hard habit to break.
- Some topics you know you should delegate are relaxing and comforting, and they provide you with a refreshing break. They are more like hobbies than work.
- You may want to feel indispensable, and delegating proves others can do some of your work. The problem with this approach is that indispensable people can't be promoted because their jobs can't be filled.
- You may feel guilty about overloading your staff.

To properly delegate, you must think about what you are trying to accomplish and what work needs to be done to achieve your objective. This takes time, and if you put it off too long, it will be too late to delegate.

As Harriet Hopf, professor and executive coach, says:

> "If you are a procrastinator, by the time you are ready to delegate, it is due tomorrow and you have no choice but to do it yourself."

If you are still having trouble delegating, start by assuming you will delegate everything. Then, only take on work that obviously requires your time and attention. To test whether this is the case, ask yourself the following questions:

- What about this situation requires my unique and specific involvement?
- Why is my staff incapable of handling this on their own?
- What should I do now so it will be easier to delegate such work in the future?

MAIN POINTS IN THIS CHAPTER

- Anything that can be delegated must be delegated.
- You can't say "Yes!" until you learn to say "No."
- Your time has real value. Treat it as such.
- The leadership agenda clarifies high- and low-value uses of your time.
- "I can do it better and faster myself" is a terrible approach to getting work done.
- When you truly delegate a topic, it comes off your to-do list. When you kind-of delegate a topic, it stays on your list.

CHAPTER 5: CREATING ALIGNMENT BY USING GIVENS

"All head coaches think they are great communicators, but rarely does anyone else think that."

Terry Pettit (former Nebraska volleyball coach)

TOOL: GIVENS CLEARLY DEFINE WHAT IS BEING DELEGATED

Givens are sentence-long statements that define the work being delegated. They define boundaries that prevent work from going too far off the mark. Within the boundaries, however, givens unleash the creativity of the person doing the work.

Once staff members understand the givens, it becomes much easier for a leader to let go of a delegated task. In the absence of givens, you have your assumptions and the person you are delegating to has theirs, and theirs might be entirely different from yours. If this is the case, you may be talking, but you are not communicating.

As an example of the power of givens to clearly define what you are looking for, suppose you told a realtor you wanted to move to their city and needed a place to live. If that was all the information you gave, there is no way the realtor could come up with a short list of possibilities that would make sense to you. But if you added just a small number of givens, it would be relatively easy for the realtor to sort through the possibilities and develop a short list that met your needs.

For example, suppose you had the following givens:

- We need to be within a 25-minute commute to downtown.
- We prefer the southern suburbs.
- We are looking to buy, not rent.
- Our budget is $X.
- We are only considering a single-family detached home.
- Our jobs have already started, so we would like to make an offer and close on the house as quickly as possible.

Any competent realtor could take these givens and identify 5–10 homes that would fit your criteria. Before the givens, it was impossible to delegate your home search. After the givens, you can delegate the initial sorting to your realtor and focus on making your choice from the list of prescreened homes the realtor develops.

EXAMPLES OF GIVENS IN VOLLEYBALL

Consider this task: deal with the T-shirts for your booster club. If the coach employs givens, they can effectively delegate this task with confidence that the result will meet their expectations.

If the task is being delegated to a seasoned and trusted person, the coach may provide a single given such as "deal with the booster club T-shirts." If the person doing the task has some familiarity with it but is less experienced, additional givens may be required. For that person, the givens may also include "identify the number of each size we need now and for the entire year."

If the person is just starting out or has not yet earned your trust, you may need to provide a more detailed set of givens, starting with the above and adding:

- Order the shirts by this Friday.
- Check with marketing for the logo and color scheme.
- Use the same fabric as last year but change the color.
- Charge them to the marketing budget.
- We need delivery by the 30th of this month.

Even this list may or may not be enough for a "C" performer. If you can't trust the work will be done properly after you have specified it with as clear a set of givens as you can, you have a personnel problem, not a givens problem.

As another example, suppose you wanted to delegate a portion of your practice planning. The following set of givens might provide a good start:

- Design a few drills focusing on communication, serving, and passing.
- Develop 2–3 variations so we can keep it fresh.
- Have your portion of the practice plan ready to review two hours before today's practice so we can finalize it together and clarify everyone's responsibilities.

Givens can also be used to describe messages you are sending to your staff and team. For example, a scouting report contains data and opinions about the opposition's tendencies. The insights arising from the report could be presented in the form of givens and might look like this:

- The outside hitter #7 virtually never hits roll shots. Defensive players should be prepared for hard hits and ready to pursue balls off the block.
- Opponent middle blockers do not move well laterally. Setters, run our offense to the pins and push tempo to stress the opponent's defense.
- Their starting middle blocker is out with an ankle injury. Until the replacement shows they can score on quick sets to the middle, pin blockers load and be great on outside hitters.

HIGHER-AND LOWER-LEVEL GIVENS

Higher-level givens are unchanging and apply to every decision within a program. They represent the core values that guide the decisions and behaviors of the entire organization. For example, Beth's three-part program vision—winning at the highest level, learning lifelong lessons and becoming a lifelong learner, and having a team that loves, trusts, and respects each other—are high-level givens that apply to every decision in her program.

Alignment with higher-level givens is critical if the head coach is going to delegate and empower assistants. As an example, if an assistant's priority is training, and the vision of the program values having a team that loves, trusts, and respects each other, the focus on a high amount of practice hours cannot supersede the need to carve out time for team building activities focused on trust and respect. Higher-level givens keep everyone pointed in the same direction and prevents people from going rogue.

Lower-level givens apply only to the specific task or project for which they were developed. The givens in the t-shirt, practice planning, and training examples above are examples of lower-level givens since they apply only to those specific decision.

CREATING CLEAR AND EFFECTIVE GIVENS

For givens to be effective, they must be explicit and clear enough that people can either agree or disagree with them. If a given is vague, it is useless. People could agree on a vague given but disagree on the underlying beliefs because there is a wide range for interpreting what that given means.

For example, suppose you have a task of measuring how high your athletes can jump. You could declare a given of "use appropriate technology to measure jump heights," but that would be a waste of time.

This given is useless for two reasons. First, does anyone want to advocate for using inappropriate technology? Second, two people could agree with the given but have different underlying beliefs about what "appropriate technology" for measuring jump heights means.

One person might say "Yes, we should use appropriate technology and use Bluetooth-enabled VERT accelerometers with the associated app to monitor the height and number of our athletes' jumps." Another person might say "Yes, we should use appropriate technology and go old-school by chalking up their fingertips and seeing how high they can make a mark on the wall."

PHRASE GIVENS EXPLICITLY

The most interesting aspect of givens is that it is less important that they are correct than that they are explicit. If you are explicit, people will understand what you are saying. They may agree or disagree, and that will lead to a good conversation about the specifics of the situation and the goals you are hoping to achieve. Explicit givens, even if they are wrong to begin with, force a conversation about what the correct approach should be. The initial givens can be corrected and restated later on to take advantage of what you learned.

It is tempting to play it safe with givens to ensure that no one is offended by them, but this waters them down and reduces their usefulness. If you are ever in doubt, make givens more provocative rather than less. Think of it as waving the red flag in front of the bull to create a reaction. It is the conversation and reaction that the givens stimulate that bring focus and energy to a project or a task.

Here are a few examples:

DON'T SAY	INSTEAD, SAY
• We want to keep our donors happy.	• Come up with a list of perks that will entice our donors to continue their support of our program.
• Work with marketing to get more fans in the arena.	• Find a way to increase per-match attendance before the end of the first round of conference play.

• Work on increasing our players' vertical jumps.	• We are stagnant in our jump height improvement. Make adjustments to the training plan so our players are jumping at least an inch higher by the postseason.

Table 5-1: Examples of explicit givens

The phrasings on the right side are clear, explicit, and provocative. They focus in on what the true underlying issues and concerns are, and by so doing, make it easier to identify and solve the right problems.

START WITH STATEMENTS, END WITH GIVENS

On a simple task, like the booster club T-shirts or the practice planning examples above, you might be able to sit down and directly write out the givens.

For a more complex and ongoing project, however, it is difficult to simply write a set of givens and have them be correct the first time. The process of creating givens for these more complex projects begins by working with your staff to brainstorm a list of statements that describe the situation you are facing. After you have developed your statements, you will be ready to step back and define your givens.

Suppose for example, you are developing your recruiting strategy with your staff. You might list out statements such as these on a whiteboard:

- It has been more than a decade since our program was set up this well for success.
- We have two scholarships available this year, and three for next year.
- We could award the scholarships to walk-ons who have proven their worth, to transfers, to incoming first years, or to international players.
- We feel obligated to do something for our walk-ons, two of whom are now in our rotation.
- We have had some interest from transfers and international players, but none of the players who have contacted us so far would greatly improve our team.
- Our weakest position is at outside hitter, and we have no entering first years or current team members who will materially change this.
- There is quite a bit of drama developing on the team because some of our walk-ons are getting more playing time than our scholarship players. The walk-ons feel they should be getting scholarships, and the scholarship players feel they should be getting playing time.

These statements help you understand the situation, but do not yet provide the guidance that flows from a set of givens. Is the goal to win it all this year? To reduce the drama by giving scholarships to the walk-ons? Here are two potential sets of givens. They are contradictory, and the head coach needs to choose one or the other. Depending on which set the coach chooses, the work for the staff will be entirely different.

Given set #1:

- We are going all in to win this year.

- Our weakness is outside hitters, and we don't see the answer coming from anyone currently on or entering the team.
- We will use all of our recruiting effort to find an outside hitter through the transfer portal or through unsigned international players.

If given set #1 was selected, the work of the staff would be external. They would look outside the current team to find an outside hitter from somewhere else. Finding this player might be difficult, but the marching orders are clear.

Alternatively, the head coach could choose given set #2:

- We owe a debt to our walk-ons who have stepped up so powerfully during their time with us.
- We will use our scholarships this year to reward the walk-ons who have earned their place in the starting lineup.
- We need to deal with the drama and the cultural issues that have developed between some of the scholarship players and the walk-ons.

Should given set #2 be selected, the focus would be internal. The work would be to award scholarships to current players and to identify and work on cultural issues.

Choosing which set of givens is most effective is a judgment call. The right set of givens will speed and improve decision-making. The wrong set of givens will reduce the probability of success even before the work has started.

TOOL: QUALITY COMMITMENTS

Quality commitments are a set of givens between someone making a request and someone accepting the request. A quality commitment has givens in three areas:

- The work to be done and the quality level required.
- The deadline for completion of the work.
- The degree of flexibility (if any) in fulfilling the request.

Once made, the quality commitment is in place until:

- It is completed to the satisfaction of the person who made the request,
- The requester withdraws their request, or
- The person who committed backs out of the commitment. (This may bring consequences to the person who did not deliver what they had promised.)

Creating a quality commitment ensures everyone will understand what is being asked for and will be able to agree on whether or not the work was completed as required.

EXAMPLES OF QUALITY COMMITMENTS

Here are three examples of quality commitments:

Example 1: Sending an assistant to the annual American Volleyball Coaches Association (AVCA) convention at the site of the NCAA Final Four.

- The assistant will attend and actively engage at the annual AVCA convention. This means not just being in the city, but attending presentations, demonstrations, and social events to build their network.

- Registration and travel arrangements must be completed at least one month before the convention in order to take advantage of the early discounts and cheaper travel.
- Attending the convention is an opportunity for professional development and should only be missed in an emergency.

Example 2: Hiring a new assistant coach

- We need to hire a new assistant coach. To do so, we will reach out to our peers in other programs and search for recommendations to develop a short list of those to be considered.
- We will make the decision by the end of March.
- This will require our full attention and we must get it done no matter what.

Example 3: Choosing a special event for the players

- Our players have been working hard and are getting to the point of needing a break. We need to craft something they would see as a special event to reward them for their efforts.
- We need to do this before the preseason ends.
- We don't have this in our budget, and so it will require a donor to sponsor it. If we can't find a donor, we may need to delay or reduce the scope of the event.

The better the quality commitments, the better the communication. As Mary Wise, Florida volleyball coach, says:

"The better I am at communicating, the better the production by our staff."

THE TWO MAIN TYPES OF WORK:
TASKS AND PROJECTS

The work you delegate can be divided into two categories: tasks and projects. Tasks are smaller, clearly defined pieces of work that can be fully delegated and removed from your to-do list. Projects are larger and more complex pieces of work and will require your continued involvement. Projects require creativity, thought, and engagement. Tasks should simply be completed and crossed off someone's list.

For a task, the head coach starts the effort off by providing the givens to the staff member. They should only come back to the head coach before the task has been completed if there are specific questions or issues. The staff member executes the task, makes decisions on their own if necessary, and then informs the leader that the task has been finished.

If it is a long task, it is a good practice for the workers to let the head coach know periodically that everything is on track. This is not a detailed update on the task, but just a quick way to let the head coach know things are moving forward.

The workflow for a task looks like this:

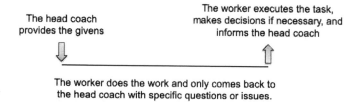

Figure 5-1: Task workflow

If a worker continually tries to engage the head coach during the task with questions and updates, the worker is not doing their job. They are either not yet capable of doing the assigned work, or are showing off to impress the head coach with how hard they have been working.

Projects are more complex and usually last longer than tasks. Unlike tasks, projects require periodic engagement between the leader and the staff members(s).

Rather than pushing ahead until the project is finished as they would for a task, staff periodically meet with the head coach along the way while working on a project. The staff present their findings, issues, and questions, and the head coach engages them with questions and provides them with further guidance. Then, the staff do more work and return for more engagement. At the conclusion of the project, the staff present their recommendations to the head coach, who makes the decision.

The workflow of a project looks like this:

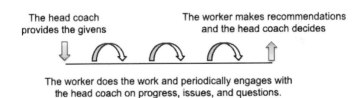

Figure 5-2: Project workflow

THE DANGER OF CONFUSING TASKS AND PROJECTS

If a head coach defines a piece of work as a task but then treats it like a project, it will waste both their time and the workers' time due to unnecessary updates and information transfers. This will make the worker appear as if they can't handle what they should be able to manage, and it will make the head coach seem like a micromanager who is unable to let go of even the smallest item.

If the head coach defines a piece of work as a project but then treats it like a task, they will not fulfill their role because projects, by definition, require engagement by the head coach.

The same exact work may be a task for a trusted and experienced staff member and a project for someone new to the program who has earned less trust and requires more guidance. This is particularly important to think about in athletics with its high turnover rate.

In athletics, there is always a new person who needs to be brought up to speed. The high turnover rate makes delegating more difficult, which means effective systems, clearly defined processes, and accessible storehouses of knowledge are critical for success.

TIPS FOR LEADING PROJECTS

Large projects (such as recruiting) may be broken down into smaller projects and tasks such as evaluation, communication, material and graphics, visits, etc. Completing these might require involvement from multiple levels of the organization at different times and in different roles. By breaking a large project down into pieces, the work is phased and becomes more manageable.

Projects and tasks for recruiting may have multiple leaders working at different levels. For example, at Utah, Beth engages regularly on the status of their recruiting program and top recruits. Dan Corotan, Utah volleyball assistant coach, leads the day-to-day activities for all recruits. The entire staff meets weekly to stay on top of the large and complex project and its associated tasks.

A person could be the leader on one project and the worker on another. For example, Malia Shoji, University of Utah volleyball associate head coach, is the leader of the Volleyball Performance Team. On the other hand, Malia is the worker on a project evaluating VERT vs. Catapult jump measurement technology. Beth is the leader on the VERT vs. Catapult project because it involves budgetary considerations and she is the one who will make the final decision.

GAME-TIME DECISIONS

There is another category of work that doesn't fall into the category of either project or task. That is game-time or in-the-moment decisions.

When you call a time-out after the opposition has scored two points in a row late in the fifth set, you are not dealing with a project or a task. Instead, you are looking for immediate recommendations so you can decide on a plan of action before the time-out ends.

When staff huddle together to talk during the time-out, they have 90 seconds to analyze what is happening, come up with alternatives, make recommendations, decide on a plan, and then inform the team. The decision-making is driven by what the staff have seen from previous matches, what they know about their own team and how they think they will respond, how the flow of the game is going, what the stats are telling them, and what they believe about the opposing players and coaches.

These decisions are at the heart of coaching, and there are few business ideas or tools that will add insight above and beyond what your coaching experience has already taught you.

TOOL: TELL LESS, KNOW MORE

There is a simple rule for effective interactions on both tasks and projects:

"Tell less, know more."

There are two approaches to show your mastery of a topic. The first is to show how much you know about it by telling everything up front. Using this approach, the more facts, ideas, and opinions you have, the greater your mastery.

The second approach is to show that you know what is important and what is not. When you follow this approach, you do not try to pass on everything you know. Instead, you pass on what is important, and hold off on the rest. Taking this approach shows you have put thought into what matters rather than simply sharing everything you know and asking the head coach to figure out what it all means.

The "tell less, know more" approach actually requires more mastery and understanding than does the "telling everything up front" approach. You may know fifty things about a topic, but it requires additional insight to identify which three of those matter the most for decision-making.

As Jay Debertin, CEO of CHS, says:

> "In a big company, the days are short. You don't have as much time to spend on any single topic as you might wish. The bright people can answer my questions in a concise, clear manner rather than telling me everything they know."

The time and attention of your leaders and staff is the most precious commodity you have. A 3-minute overview that hits the main points will impress your head coach far more than a 15-minute presentation jam-packed with random facts and unimportant details. When you show you have sufficient mastery to know what matters, you will build confidence and trust with those above you.

Take a look at the upright and inverted pyramids:

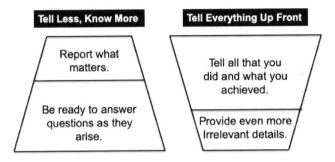

Figure 5-3: Tell less, know more

The upright pyramid on the left shows how to best engage with your leaders. Start by reporting what matters, and then add more as they ask questions. If you have a 15-minute meeting, keep the report to 3-minutes so there is plenty of time to answer questions and jointly work the problem.

The inverted pyramid on the right leads to boredom, frustration, and reduced confidence in the staff person's abilities. The staff person is not trying to efficiently present the information to their leader, they are trying to impress their leader with their cleverness and hard work by telling them all they know and everything they did. In a 15-minute meeting, they would babble on for 12 minutes before the leader would finally be able to interrupt and enter the conversation.

The "tell less, know more" rule applies to candidates inter-viewing for a job as well. How many times have you interviewed a candidate and were never able to break into the conversation because they simply would not stop talking? Candidates who get hired talk a little bit about themselves, and then engage in a con-versation about the issues that concern you. Those that talk on and on will find it much more difficult to get the job to which they aspire.

Just as you want your people to "tell less, know more," you want to do exactly the same thing with your boss. Athletics is highly visible in the community, and the last thing you need is to have a reporter ask your athletic director (AD) about something that you have not told them. Your AD does not need to know all of the details, but they need to know what is important, and they certainly do not want to be surprised. Particularly if it is bad news, it is better your AD hear about it from you rather than from any other source.

Whether you are dealing with your boss or your subordinates, get in the habit of telling less and knowing more. When bosses hear you tell less and know more, they develop a sense that you know what matters and that you have things under control. When your subordinates hear you tell less and know more, they see that you believe in the power of doing so and it will become easier for them to follow your lead.

MAIN POINTS IN THIS CHAPTER

- Givens enhance communication and align a program from top to bottom.
- Givens should be clear, explicit, and provocative.
- Higher-level givens are applied to all decisions within

a program. Lower-level givens are relevant only for the specific decision for which they were created.

- Quality commitments enable accountability.
- Tasks and projects are different types of work and require different interactions between the head coach and the workers.
- Always tell less and know more.

CHAPTER 6: DEVELOPING EFFECTIVE STAFF MEMBERS

"It is hard to be direct with adults. It is easier with your players. And since staff wear regular clothes, it is hard to know by looking at them who is an All-American staff member."

Tara VanDerveer (Stanford women's basketball coach)

YOUR STAFFING PHILOSOPHY

Every head coach should begin by developing their staffing philosophy. Karch Kiraly, head coach of the USA women's national volleyball team, summed up his staffing philosophy in this way:

> "I am not as concerned about their skill level when they enter the program. I want people who are hungry to grow and who are good learners."

Patrick Lencioni, business author whose 11 books have sold six million copies, has a different staffing philosophy. In his book *The Ideal Team Player*, he states that the three virtues you want in a staff member are being humble, hungry, and smart. A humble person cares more about the success of the team than the credit they receive. A hungry person has a strong work ethic and is motivated to do ever more to contribute to their team's success. Being a smart person is less about having a high IQ and more about possessing good judgement and being effective in dealing with others.

Factors to consider in developing your own staffing philosophy include:

- How long do you want your assistants to stay? Are you seeing them as long-term partners or as five-year team members who will then be moving on to their own head coaching position?
- Are you focusing on raising the floor of your assistants or on raising their ceilings? In other words, will you be more focused on bringing them up to solid performance (their floor) or unleashing their full capabilities (their ceilings)?
- How much responsibility will you delegate, and how long will you give your staff to prove they are ready for more?

Your staffing philosophy balances what is good for the program vs. what is good for the assistant. For example, you may have an assistant who is great at practice planning but doesn't follow up well on recruiting. For the good of the program, you might be tempted to keep that person on practice planning indefinitely so you can reap the benefit of their strength in that area. But by doing so, you may stand in the way of their developing the well-rounded skills they will need to become a head coach. And if they don't test the full range of their skills out, they might not even know themselves whether they want to, or are capable of, advancing to a head coaching role.

ALIGNING AND MOTIVATING YOUR STAFF

Your staff need to know they are part of something great and that they can make a meaningful contribution to the program. They need to believe in your culture and be energized by the high-level givens that define your program's vision.

Amy Hogue, University of Utah softball head coach, described her view of culture this way:

> "Create a culture you are proud of and then find a way to compete to win games."

Instill the high-level givens that define your vision as soon as you can. At the latest, this is a conversation to be had on their first day on the job. Better still, make sure candidates know your vision during the interview process so they understand what they would be getting themselves into should they join your program.

While the head coach is accountable for everything within the program, they do not have to be in charge of everything. Beth divides work to be led by each assistant and makes sure each assistant is in charge of something that matters to the program. Delegating big areas of responsibility to assistants shows them they are an important piece of the puzzle and that you have confidence in them.

As an example, recruiting is its own entity and is often the sole responsibility of one assistant. Because recruiting is such a large grouping of tasks and projects, the assistant in charge has the opportunity to put their mark on this highly valued area of the program. Assistants have the authority to delegate work from their assigned areas of responsibilities, and can even delegate small but necessary tasks back to their head coach. Giving assistants the lead both gives them pride in their area and spreads out the massive amount of work.

Jay Debertin, CEO of CHS, told us:

> "If you bring the right people around you, they will figure it out. They are more competitive within themselves than due to pressure from someone else. No one can put more pressure on them than they put on themselves."

After a successful season in 2014, both of Beth's assistants left to become head coaches at other universities. Beth had never turned over two assistants in the same year, and it raised new challenges since she would not have an experienced assistant to help the new person. This meant the assistants had to come to Beth for advice on relatively simple tasks that an experienced assistant would have been able to handle quite easily by themselves.

The experience wasn't there, but the passion and energy certainly were. The two new assistants brought in new ideas and concepts, many of which were incorporated into the program. There were many changes that year, and it was exciting to watch skilled and motivated, if inexperienced, assistant coaches revamping old strategies and creating new ones in collaboration with Beth.

GIVE YOUR STAFF ROOM TO BREATHE

Sometimes the best course of action is to avoid trying to solve every problem. You need to give your staff room to breathe. As

John Dunning, American Volleyball Coaches Association Hall of Famer, told us:

> "Everything that confronts you doesn't need a solution—just be a listener."

If you are continually in problem-solving mode, your staff won't get the space they need to create solutions. Just listening often elicits creative and game-changing insights from staff members. It also opens a channel in which staff members feel they can share issues with you without the fear of being micromanaged. In addition, it will instill in them the valuable habit of always brainstorming potential solutions before bringing you a problem that needs solving.

THE DANGER OF BECOMING TOO GOOD AT ONLY ONE THING

Staff development is a primary goal for any coach. Terry Pettit, former Nebraska volleyball coach, says:

> "Talent is something someone arrives with. Skill can be trained."

Preparing an assistant to be ready to be a head coach requires a balance of leveraging their strengths to help your program and giving them time to work on improving their weaknesses to help in their own careers. If you let them spend too much time on their strengths and not enough time on shoring up their weaknesses, their career can stall out. They will not develop the broad range of skills required to advance to the next level.

As an example, Leo had an associate at his consulting firm who was spectacular at financial modeling. He was so good that partners lined up to have him build the models they required to analyze their clients' decisions. After three years of steady modeling work, however, he had reached a point in his career at which he should have been doing less modeling and more leading of client teams.

The other associates who were hired at the same time had experienced a wide variety of work on their projects, and all of them were ready to lead client teams. But the modeler was not yet ready to lead teams because all his experience was focused on developing his modeling skills. Because he lacked the necessary all-around skills, he was viewed as not being ready for promotion and more responsibility.

That example is similar to keeping an assistant coach who is outstanding at training but lacking in the other skills necessary to become a successful head coach. That person adds significant value to the program through their ability to teach and run drills and could be happy doing that exclusively, but should recognize they might not be developing the skills that would enable them to take over their own program.

Karch Kiraly, USA women's national volleyball team coach, addressed this when he told us:

> "I am less apt to shift major responsibilities—they have to be masters at what they do."

This is true at the highest levels of international competition. For most programs, though, this raises the trade-off. Do you shift responsibilities so your people develop well-rounded capabilities, or do you focus them on only one or two things so they develop mastery?

Ways to build skills in your staff include:

- Sharing what has made you successful. Don't hold back on the "Secret Sauce" that has propelled your career.
- Having them attend regional and national coaching conferences so they can build their professional networks.
- Preventing your staff from becoming too comfortable. Once they have mastered a skill or area, assign them to something new.
- Providing them with opportunities for promotion or advancement so that they never feel their job is stagnant or that they have to leave your program to expand their opportunities or increase their income.
- Making development discussions part of staff meetings. One possibility is to assign readings on a rotating basis to summarize and discuss.

We recommend setting SMART goals for your staff. SMART goals are: Specific; Measurable; Actionable; Relevant; and Timely. An example of a smart goal is to "increase perfect pass percentage by one percent in the coming month." This statement covers each part of a smart goal:

- Specific: Perfect passes is a measure used by the team.
- Measurable: We normally track this statistic and can compare the improved performance to historical performance.
- Actionable: We can spend more time at practice on passing and use passing-specific drills.
- Relevant: Passing is correlated to winning.
- Timely: If we can do it within one month, we will be ready for the upcoming postseason tournament.

TOOL: THE DISC BEHAVIORAL MODEL

DISC stands for Dominance, Influence, Conscientiousness, and Steadiness. Each person has a different weighting of these four behavioral styles, and each style brings its own contributions to team success. Utah uses the DISC behavioral model to explore and define the way each member of its team prefers to behave in different situations. DISC leads to in-depth conversations about how people are different, the strengths they bring, and how different behavioral types can work together to create a winning team.

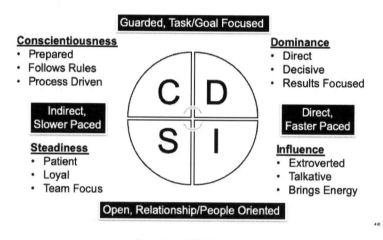

Guarded, Task/Goal Focused

Conscientiousness
• Prepared
• Follows Rules
• Process Driven

Dominance
• Direct
• Decisive
• Results Focused

Indirect, Slower Paced

Direct, Faster Paced

C | D
S | I

Steadiness
• Patient
• Loyal
• Team Focus

Influence
• Extroverted
• Talkative
• Brings Energy

Open, Relationship/People Oriented

Figure 6-1: DISC framework

Dominance brings directness, decisiveness, and the ability to focus on achieving outstanding results. Influence brings extroverted, talkative, and energetic behaviors. Steadiness brings patience, loyalty, and a focus on what is best for the team. Conscientiousness brings preparation and a focus on rules and process.

When all of these are represented on the team, the necessary pieces to win are in place. By understanding each member's preferred behavioral style and by being transparent about the results, everyone will understand each other's style and be able to communicate more effectively.

APPLYING THE DISC BEHAVIORAL MODEL

As an example of an application of DISC, Beth had a player a few years ago with whom she struggled to connect. Beth could not teach this player without the player getting frustrated. Off the court they were fine, but in a practice or match situation, there was always tension. Beth wasn't sure why this was the case until the DISC tool provided her with an insight she had not previously understood.

Beth is an I/S in DISC, which is relationship based and fast paced, and the "I," which is her strongest style, meant she is an influencer. Once Beth learned that this player was in the "C" profile, which includes rule followers, analytical and process-driven people, she quickly understood the problem.

Beth realized this player would do better if they had time to internalize the feedback and process it. Beth started pulling the player aside to explain the feedback in detail, and then gave them time on a different court to work it out. When the player came back to the main court, they felt more confident and appreciated that they could take time to process the feedback and that the coach cared enough to understand their style.

Since both staff and players use the DISC tool, it is diverse in its usage. Players can use it to connect better with their teammates. Staff can use it to communicate better with their players. And staff can use it amongst themselves to improve their understanding and appreciation of one another. The Utah program works with a company called Athlete Assessments (www.athleteassessments. com) which specializes in tailoring DISC to the needs of athletics.

There are numerous other models of behavioral types, including the Myers-Briggs Type Indicator (MBTI) and the Enneagram of Personality. Whichever model you choose, helping individuals understand their own style and how they differ with the styles of their colleagues and teammates will greatly enhance communication and teamwork.

GIVING EFFECTIVE FEEDBACK

Never be embarrassed about giving feedback. Be clear, direct, and honest. Feedback should be constructive, nonjudgmental, brief, timely, confidential, and focused on behaviors. If you are trained in using the DISC profile tool, you can tailor feedback to a preferred behavior style, which will accelerate learning and growth.

It is important to give your staff both positive feedback (behaviors that you would like to see repeated) and negative feedback (things you would like to see improved). You would not hesitate to point out to your players when you see something that could be improved or that would lead to bad habits if you allowed it to continue. For some reason, however, it is harder to give immediate and constructive feedback to your staff.

Too often, people are tentative with their feedback. They don't want to offend, so they will soften the feedback and present it in a roundabout way. But if you aren't clear and direct, the feedback you give may not even be heard. Harriet Hopf, professor and executive coach, told us:

"When you sugar coat feedback too much, people may not even know they are getting feedback. To put them into feedback-receiving mode, tell them 'I am going to give you feedback now.'"

One popular model is the so-called "feedback sandwich," where constructive criticism (the meat) is layered between two pieces of praise (the bread). But the positives in the bread may drown out the negatives in the meat, and overuse may erode trust and lead to individuals tuning out all feedback.

A better feedback approach is Ask-Tell-Ask-Tell. In this approach, you ask the staff member: "What went well?" After they provide examples, you tell them your observations and amplify what they said. Then ask them, "What could be improved?" After they give examples, tell them your own observations.

Remember to base your observations on behaviors so that the focus is on what they did, not who they are. It is much easier to avoid defensiveness if the focus of the feedback is on their behavior, rather than being perceived as an attack on them as a person.

TOOL: SITUATION, BEHAVIOR, IMPACT (SBI)

An effective way to focus on what they did rather than who they are is to use the Situation, Behavior, Impact (SBI) tool. Situations anchor the discussion in time and place. Behaviors are the specific, observable actions you witnessed. Impacts are the thoughts and feelings that resulted from the behaviors, including how other people were affected by them.

As an example, simply saying "you were rude and disrespectful" is not helpful. Using the SBI approach, the same comment would be expressed as: "At this morning's meeting (Situation), when you took a phone call and kept looking at your watch (Behavior), I felt like I was a low priority and was frustrated that we weren't able to finish an important task (Impact)."

SBI is particularly useful for giving feedback on professionalism, communication, and attitudes and behaviors. It also works well when folded into the "Tell" portions of Ask-Tell-Ask-Tell as a way to communicate your observations.

Here are some examples:

DON'T SAY	INSTEAD, USE SBI AND SAY
We need to firm up our block.	As of today, we are second to last in the conference in blocking, and it seems we are just slower than our opponents. The drills you have been running with the middles are confusing them and are not improving their performance.
We need to get better at recruiting.	We lost our last two top recruits from our home state, and we simply are not competitive for local athletes. You haven't been communicating frequently enough with the athletes, their families, and their coaches, and that is hurting our relationships with them.
Sandy, I would like you to work a bit harder and up your game.	Sandy, at the end of today's practice you looked tired and bored. The players see you as a leader, and they modeled what you were doing and checked out of things themselves.

Great job! (Remember that feedback is positive as well!)	Today you showed up to practice well prepared and focused. Our blockers clearly made progress in improving eye work and reacting more quickly.

Table 6-1: Situation, Behavior, Impact examples

An often-ignored aspect of feedback is training your staff and players—and yourself—to become more adept at accepting and, at the next level, welcoming feedback. Feedback is often painful, and it is easy to get defensive in response. *Thanks for the Feedback: The Science and Art of Receiving Feedback Well*, by Douglas Stone and Sheila Heen, is an excellent resource for learning how to embrace both the giving and receiving of feedback.

HELPING YOUR PEOPLE TO SPEAK UP AND BE HEARD

Growth comes not just from receiving feedback, but also from learning to speak up and being heard. Just as some people give tentative, soft feedback, staff members can give quiet, timid ideas. Their ideas may be wonderful, but without the personal presence and confidence to make themselves heard, their ideas will wither and die.

Assistants often have something to say but may not be sure if it is important enough to bring forward. Beth has had many examples in which her staff members thought they were presenting ideas to her, but she didn't even understand they were trying to get her attention. Instead of being direct, they sometimes throw out partial pieces of the story to see if Beth will bite. The problem is that it may take three of four of these nuggets before Beth realizes that the assistant is trying to say something important.

Teaching your assistants to have confidence and tell the entire story will save valuable time. Beth is much more apt to listen to an idea when people come prepared with a complete and compelling story.

As an example of doing it the right way, Associate Head Coach Malia Shoji brought forth the idea of using the DISC behavioral tool and investing time and money into it. Beth had dabbled in the tool before, but had not realized its value and so had discontinued it. Malia did a deep dive into understanding the tool, spent hours researching it, and found a company that would help them get up to speed quickly. She then brought the full story to Beth. While it would have been easy for Beth to dismiss using DISC since she had already done so once before, she listened and had to admit Malia made good points. Utah adapted the DISC tool, and it has paid big dividends for the program.

BUILDING A CULTURE THAT PROMOTES SPEAKING UP

Your culture can either help people speak up or make it harder to do so. Staff may fear speaking up if their ideas are immediately dismissed or if you make them feel like they are interrupting when they try to bring something up. Your job is to create a culture in which speaking up is rewarded and even bad ideas are given a respectful hearing. When your staff speaks up, whether to call your attention to something, give you feedback, or suggest an idea, you will benefit by paying serious attention to them.

When you are in the process of making a decision, invite your staff to give their opinions before you do and listen to them without interrupting. You must let them go first since once they hear your opinion, they will feel the decision has already been made, and they will begin to support what they think you have chosen.

Karch Kiraly, USA women's national volleyball team coach, poses questions to his group and asks for their input and thoughts before he gives his opinion. This is important, because if the leader states their opinion first, everyone else will line up to support them rather than trying to think of different ways of looking at the problem.

Beth starts her planning sessions by asking the assistants what they believe the team should work on for the week. She compiles the list of ideas offered by her staff and compares their ideas to her own. By allowing her staff to voice their priorities first, their ideas are used and they feel ownership in the process.

EVALUATING YOUR STAFF

As much as your staff is part of your team, their performance still needs to be evaluated. Evaluations indicate when one of your staff members is ready for promotion, and they also identify strengths and weaknesses that can lead to ideas for growth.

Evaluations are different from day-to-day feedback. Evaluations judge and summarize someone's contribution to the program, while feedback is intended to improve their performance without judgment. While daily feedback is crucial, having a formal evaluation can be useful in summarizing ongoing contributions and setting larger goals. Think of daily feedback as quizzes and the formal evaluation as the final exam.

In business, annual evaluations are the norm. The person being evaluated first fills out a form analyzing their own performance. Their supervisor reads through the form, makes their own comments, and then the two sit down and discuss the performance together.

Because of the high turnover rate in athletics, waiting a year between evaluations doesn't make much sense. Instead, giving feedback and evaluating performance should be a part of your daily routine. Karch Kiraly, USA women's national volleyball team coach, put it this way:

> "I am not a big believer in annual reviews. We know we need to give consistent feedback to players. Why wouldn't we use that same principle with staff?"

RETAINING AND MOTIVATING YOUR STAFF

The amount of money you make is determined by the industry you are in and the level of job you hold. Different firms in the same industry pay about the same, so it simply doesn't work to say "I know we are terrible people, but we pay you more than our competitors would."

The best ways to retain and motivate your staff are the same in business and in athletics. You retain and motivate them by:

- Building a winning organization as measured by how you define winning. If your organization is winning, people will be happy. If your organization is not winning, there is almost nothing you can do to make them happy.

- Enabling your staff to learn more and faster in your organization than they could anywhere else. The more they learn, the faster they will rise. If you can credibly grow your people faster and better than other programs, you will have an edge in retaining your best people.

- Enabling your staff to live the life they want to lead. Careers are important, but so are family, friends, and outside interests. Within the constraints of the demands of your sport, the more flexibility and accommodation you can provide, the harder it will be for another program to match what you offer.

WORK/LIFE BALANCE DURING THE SEASON

The demands of coaching are intense, and there will be some times during the year when it won't feel balanced. You may need to think of work/life balance as something you get on average over the course of a year in a mix of intense periods and relatively calm ones.

During the season, for instance, a coach has very little independent or negotiable time. There is a rhythm to the season and each week is extremely task heavy. There are no shortcuts to:

- Review video of your team to plan practices for the upcoming week.
- Tag video for your players to watch.
- Watch video of your upcoming opponents to put together two scouting plans by Thursday.
- Keep your recruiting contacts going.
- Make plans for travel and being on the road every other week.

There is very little variation possible while keeping the machine churning week after week in your attempt to defeat opponents that are working just as hard as you are. And in the Pac-12, there is a good chance that one or both of your opponents each week will be ranked in the top 25 nationally.

With that said, it is critical to carve out a few moments for yourself in order to recharge and relax. Activities such as workouts, meditation, or naps go a long way towards enabling you to sustain the pace the season demands.

WORK/LIFE BALANCE DURING THE OFF-SEASON

During the off-season, recruiting travel is heavy. You need to take time to review, analyze, and develop insights from the previous season's performances. You must plan your spring training program. You need to invest time into personal player development, including their academics. You need to plan the competitive schedule for the following season. And you also need to prepare for summer camps. There is a huge amount of work to do, but you have more choice as to when to do it. You are not locked-in to a fixed schedule as you are during the season.

Beth preaches the importance of balance to her staff and encourages them to take care of their physical and mental health, particularly in the off-season. Getting young assistants to internalize this is hard, but Beth is relentless, as she herself has not always been the best at balance. She tells her staff to come in a little later if they want to, take a day off now and again, take care of personal appointments, spend time with their families, and take vacations. In general, the off-season is a time to rejuvenate so you come back ready for the rigors of the season.

Some collegiate volleyball programs use members of the same coaching staff for indoor volleyball in the fall and for outdoor beach volleyball in the spring. Coaches covering both of these seasons will be hard pressed to define an off-season and will be especially challenged to find balance in their professional and personal lives.

SHOWING APPRECIATION TO YOUR STAFF

Everyone wants to feel valued and that their hard work and dedication has been noticed, appreciated, and rewarded. While head coaches often have a results-based bonus structure in their contract, assistants do not, or even if they do, the amount they can earn in bonuses is much smaller than the head coach's.

But there are many ways of giving nonfinancial rewards. Assistants can be rewarded by:

- Acknowledging their good work privately.
- Highlighting their work publicly to the team or to the media.
- Recognizing your recruiting coordinators efforts if the team's recruiting class is ranked highly in national publications.
- Celebrating statistical success in an area that the assistant oversees.
- Receiving positive feedback from players.

As Tara VanDerveer, Stanford women's basketball coach, said:

"I have always understood the importance of letting people know I appreciate their hard work, but I am expressing it even more now."

MAIN POINTS IN THIS CHAPTER

- Begin by developing your staffing philosophy.
- Manage your staff, but give them room to breathe.
- Giving effective feedback can be learned and must be practiced. Ask-Tell-Ask-Tell and SBI are helpful tools for giving feedback.
- The DISC tool (or other behavioral typing tools) helps staff and players communicate in ways that are effective for each individual.
- You will need to help your staff to stand up and be heard.
- Work/life balance is important and requires effort.
- You can never show too much appreciation to your staff.

CHAPTER 7: HIRING AND TRAINING YOUR STAFF

"For a staff to succeed, everyone needs to be willing to check their egos at the door and strive for the same results."

Tom Farden (Utah gymnastics coach)

PROFESSIONALISM NEEDS TO BE TAUGHT

Jill Hirschinger, former UNH volleyball coach, told us:

"Volleyball is a very social sport. When you have really young assistants just out of college, they struggle with the role of being a coach or friend."

Particularly if a new staff member played for you, it is challenging to transition existing peer relationships with the players to the more formal role of coaching staff. Thus, new staff need specific training in professionalism in coaching. A good lesson to learn for young assistants is that their relationships with players are built for the betterment of the team, not just to make friends or to be liked. There will come a time when the young staff member will need to look your players in the eye and say "I am not your friend. I am your coach."

Young staff may not be used to working in an office environment. Basics such as showing up on time, dressing appropriately, knowing when to put away your cell phone, and properly interacting with older and more experienced coaches must be taught. At a higher level, their interactions with recruits, fans, and athletics administration will all be more effective and enjoyable if approached with respectful professionalism. If you assume everyone naturally knows how to do this, you will inevitably be disappointed.

Professionalism includes being trustworthy. A coach needs to be transparent, loyal, and not secretive. Young assistants often struggle with what is important enough to bring to the head coach and what is not. If there is any doubt, always tell the head coach.

IF ONE STAFF MEMBER KNOWS, ALL STAFF MEMBERS KNOW

Beth has a policy that all staff members in her program understand. If something is shared with one staff member, all staff members will know about it. This means assistants cannot have secrets from each other or from the head coach. It can be a difficult situation to navigate, and there will be errors in judgement, but assistants must learn this rule if they are to be successful in the coaching profession.

Athletes will challenge this policy, often playing one coach off of another. In non-technical terms, this translates as: "If one parent says no, then go ask the other." While players need to know they can trust staff members, they cannot be allowed to find solace from one staff member at the expense of healthy functioning relationships with the rest of the staff.

Sometimes a player tells an assistant something with the hope it will be shared with the head coach. The best thing an assistant can do in that situation is to tell that player to go directly to the head coach themselves. This ensures both that the communication is clear and unfiltered, and that the player learns how to hold, rather than how to avoid, difficult or uncomfortable conversations. The bottom line is that loyalty to the program trumps all other loyalties, as long as the program rules are being followed and no one is engaging in unethical behavior.

STAFF NORMS

Beth has developed a set of staff norms which can be thought of as givens for staff behavior and professionalism. These include:

- Lead by example and enforce the culture of the program. Being neutral does not enhance the culture, and it is not just the head coach's responsibility to create the culture. It is the job of the assistants and leaders of the team as well.
- Confidentiality is critical so that staff members feel confident when discussing challenging topics and issues.
- Support fellow staff members even when mistakes are made.
- Loyalty goes to the program, not to one staff member or player.
- 24-Hour Rule: If an issue arises, discuss it within a day, or let it go.

- All perspectives are respected, needed, and valued.
- More information is better than less. Don't let the head coach be surprised.
- Once a decision has been made, staff should stop debating it. The team will receive only one unified message.
- Come prepared to meetings, be on time, and do not be on your cell phone unless it is related to the meeting topic.
- Come to meetings with potential solutions to problems (be proactive).
- It is important and professional to respond to phone calls, texts, and emails. Texts should be responded to within an hour, emails within a day. If it is after hours and something is not critically important, send an email rather than a text.
- Take care of yourself and your family (physically, mentally, and emotionally).

ASSEMBLING YOUR STAFF

Numerous questions and trade-offs arise as you select your staff. Are you looking for experience or are you willing to take a chance on someone just starting out? Are you looking for the best possible person or for someone who fills in the gaps of your current staff? How important is culture and attitude compared to raw ability? How does their pace and energy fit with what your program needs? How much do they already know about your sport, and how hungry are they to learn more?

It is also critical to understand that excellent leaders are not threatened by those who have skills they lack. In the words of

Mary Wise, Florida volleyball coach:

> "Today I have a much better understanding of MY
> weaknesses. Now that I understand that, I have
> learned to hire people who are great at the things I
> am not. From there, it is my job to provide the big
> picture required for our program's success and then
> get out of their way."

You will never find a candidate who is the best at everything and who answers all of your questions. You need to prioritize what matters and accept that the best candidate may only deliver 80% of what you seek. If you wait for a 100% candidate, your position will go unfilled until it is too late and you will end up scrambling to find a 60% candidate.

Few people enter coaching for the big money. While the money is good at the very top, the vast majority of head and assistant coaches make less money than they would in other professions. Most assistants come from the ranks of student-athletes, and coaching gives them the opportunity to stay connected to the game they love. Because of this, the people applying to your program see coaching as a calling.

JUDGING TALENT

In the movie *Miracle,* based on the 1980 USA gold medal-winning hockey team, coach Herb Brooks had this discussion with assistant coach Craig Patrick:

> Craig Patrick: You're missing the best players.

> Herb Brooks: I'm not looking for the best players,
> Craig, I'm looking for the right ones.

In the movie *The Recruit*, Al Pacino plays CIA recruiter Walter Burke and says:

> "You gotta give me one thing. I'm a scary judge of talent."

Are you a scary judge of talent? If not, what can you do to improve? No matter how wonderful you are by yourself, you cannot do the job of an entire staff. That means learning to judge, based on only a short interaction, who has the magic and who does not.

The same is true in almost any other activity. Jay Debertin, CEO of CHS, told us:

> "If there is one skill leadership has to have, it is an eye for talent."

WHY INTERVIEWING CANDIDATES TELLS YOU SO LITTLE ABOUT THEM

You were hired once, so you must have done well on your interview. But beyond your own interview, how much training have you had on how to test for fit, ability, knowledge, hunger, and attitude?

Candidates know what to expect on interviews. They know you will ask them about their previous experience and why they are interested in your program. They know you will ask them about their greatest strengths and weaknesses. They know they will be introduced to your staff and perhaps meet briefly with your athletic director. They expect to meet some of your players and may even lead a drill on court.

Because they know all of this, they come to you with their answers already worked out and rehearsed. This means you may never actually see them think on their feet. Instead, they will just spit out their preplanned acceptable and noncontroversial answers.

One way to learn more about your candidates is to shake them up and have them work through a problem. There is a tool to do this that is used by management consulting firms to separate out the people who really have what it takes from those who just look good on paper: the case study interview.

TOOL: THE CASE STUDY INTERVIEW

The purpose of a case study interview is to observe how an applicant thinks. There is no right answer, so you are not judging them on whether they are correct or not. You are judging them on how they think on their feet, how creative they are, how many different ways they can think of to attack a problem, how well they identify the issues, and how they interact with the person leading them through the case and with others in the room.

To lead a case, you first set up a situation, then ask the applicant how they would deal with it, and finally move into a discussion in which you ask probing questions to dig deeper into their ideas. Sometimes the head coach leads the case, while other times they want someone else to lead it so they can focus on observing the applicant.

Applicants are allowed to ask questions during the case, but surprisingly, many don't. If they do ask a question, you answer it and then let them continue. If they start to slow down or get off track, you ask probing questions to delve deeper into their thinking and to get them refocused on the topic.

An applicant who does well on a case will engage you in a conversation, and it will feel more like a working session than an interview. An applicant who does poorly will keep running into dead ends and will be unable to think of different approaches to get themselves unstuck.

Beth and Leo teamed up to run applicants for an assistant coach position through case studies that were based on real issues the Utah program had recently faced. Since Leo had run hundreds of case interviews, he led these sessions so that Beth could spend most of her time observing.

CHOOSING TOPICS FOR THE CASE STUDY INTERVIEW

We ran four 30-minute case studies during the day-long interviews for each of the candidates who had made the short list based on their resumes, recommendations, and experience. Two of the cases involved only Leo and the candidate with Beth and associate head coach Malia Shoji observing. The other two cases were done in a group consisting of the candidate, Beth, and Shoji.

These two approaches enabled Beth to evaluate both how well the candidate thought on their own and how they worked and interacted with the staff they would be joining. Questions Beth asked herself included: Were they deep thinkers? Were they intimidated? Were they quiet? Could they build on the ideas of others? Could they push back on the ideas of the existing staff?

Here are the two cases we used with only Leo and the applicant:

- We have the standard volleyball statistics program, Data Volley, up and running. Our previous assistant had taken the lead on this, and our former director of operations who had been running the system has also moved on. How should we gather the data we need, and how should we use the data to create value for our program?

- We have three weeks of preseason to get the team ready to play. What should we do, what resources will we need, and how should we prioritize our activities?

Here are the two group cases we used with the applicant, Beth, and Shoji working together as a team:

- The University of Utah Women's Volleyball program is placing its bet for excellence on developing a culture that is collaborative and that unites behind strong player and team development. How do we make this approach translate into winning, and what will be the keys to making it work?

- We have a discipline issue. One of our top three players has been losing focus and their work ethic has slipped. The player is a senior and is seen as a team leader. How should we handle this with the player and with the rest of the team?

At the end of the two hours of case interviews, we knew far more about how the applicant thinks and interacts than we did before the session began. And the applicant left with a much better understanding of the collaborative style of the Utah coaching staff.

AVOIDING BIASES IN HIRING AND RECRUITING

We naturally tend to gravitate to those who look, act, and think like we do and who share a similar background. But if you limit your search just to people like you, you are only looking at a narrow slice of the population.

You need to find the best people, and they may differ from you in ethnicity, religion, gender, political views, or sexual preference. You can learn to adapt to these differences and develop an appreciation for how people differ from you. What you can't adapt to are people with whom you feel comfortable but who do not bring value to your program. Finding the best people, no matter how much they differ from you, is essential to being designed to win.

THE VALUE CASE FOR DIVERSITY

Most programs try for diversity to meet targets or simply because they believe treating everyone fairly is the ethical thing to do. They may take the first step and ensure that diverse individuals get a fair shot at being hired, and they may end up hiring people who are very different from themselves. Too often, however, once they hire a more diverse workforce, they try to socialize them to act like everyone else in the organization. They seek out diversity of background and then stomp out diversity of thought.

But it is the diversity of thinking, beliefs, experiences, and approaches that allows you to create something greater than you could have achieved on your own. Beth could have looked for a mini-me who thought exactly as she does to be her co-author. They probably would have worked together smoothly, and there would have been few arguments or disagreements along the way as they would each think like the other.

But the whole point of this book is that the diversity of thinking and experiences that Beth and Leo bring is what led to growth on both sides. As Ann Northrop, journalist and gay activist, says,

> "Don't tolerate me as different. Accept me as part of the spectrum of normalcy."

You seek out diversity not because people say you should. Not because you have to make your numerical targets. You seek out diversity because having people who bring different things to the table allows you to broaden your own thinking and enables you to come up with better alternatives and more effective decisions than you could on your own.

You don't want to simply have diversity; you want inclusion so that everyone participates in designing your organization to win. As Vernā Myers, Vice President of Inclusion Strategy at Netflix, says,

> "Diversity is being asked to the party. Inclusion is being asked to dance."

DEVELOPING A KNOWLEDGE STOREHOUSE

Athletics has a high turnover rate. That means you will almost always have a new person to train. Doing so one-on-one is labor intensive, and it is just as hard to bring the second new person up to speed as it was the first. To gain efficiency and effectiveness, you need to create processes, systems, and stored knowledge that enables you to quickly train new people.

To do this, we recommend building a centralized knowledge storehouse. This prevents you from having to start from scratch with every new staff member. It also enables new staff members to partially train themselves by reading through what has been done previously.

There are three parts to an effective knowledge storehouse. First, you need to gather all of the bits and pieces of what has been done in the past into one place. Second, you need to update your stored knowledge continually as things change. And third, you need to make sure the knowledge is readily accessible to your staff. The best way to do this is by creating a searchable online knowledge database which you and your staff update as changes occur.

TOOL: THE SEARCHABLE ONLINE KNOWLEDGE DATABASE

There are several ways of keeping track of the work being done in your program. You could write all of the different pieces of work out on Post-it notes and organize them on a blank wall. You could create an Excel spreadsheet. The best approach, however, is to build a searchable online knowledge database.

You don't know how to build a database you say? Not a problem. A few years ago, you would have needed technical help and would have had to brace yourself for a steep learning curve. Now, however, you can get a web-based database up and running by yourself within an hour with little or no training.

The easiest and most user-friendly site we have found is airtable.com. You can sign up for a free account, create a database in a matter of minutes, and begin entering tasks and projects. The nice thing about a database is that you don't have to worry about having everything organized and ready before starting. You can enter tasks and projects in any order and assign names and add further detail later. The database organizes everything for you.

The Utah Utes airtable database lists 210 line items of work. These range from scheduling preseason matches, to practice planning, to organizing senior night. Large topics are broken down into individual projects and tasks. For example, recruiting is broken down into 25 line items such as prospecting and evaluating high school and club players, campus visits, etc.

Each of these pieces of work can be assigned a deadline and given to one or more staff members. In addition, you can define above- and below-the-line tasks for yourself and for every staff member so it is totally clear what has been delegated to whom. Here is a screenshot showing a small part of the Utah database:

Month	Catagory	Task Name	Person			Description
May	Camp	Camp Schedules	Dan	Kate	Liz	Review and make changes as necessary
January	Camp	Camp dates	Chloe	Kate		Set dates as soon as possible
February	Camp	Order Camp Balls	Chloe	Kate		Order Balls from Molton in Feb through Molten Contract
	Camp	Camp Administrator	Chloe	Kate		Kate Holdeman
February	Camp	Online Registration	Chloe	Kate		Create online registration Based on selected dates Info?
February	Camp	Pricing	Chloe	Kate		Sep up yearly meeting with Beth to discuss pricing Prepare before meet
February	Camp	Advertising / Mailing	Chloe	Kate		Create advertisement for camps Brochures VB Magazine Prep Volleyba
May	Camp	Housing	Chloe	Kate		Communicate dates to housing Liason Sign contracts Receive bill & get
May	Camp	Food	Chloe	Kate		Communicate with dining services Get contract and sign {include staff f
February	Camp	Facilities	Chloe	Kate		Communicate with Gavin and Brent Secure as many gyms as possible G
July	Camp	Parking/Signage	Chloe	Kate		Communicate with Gavin and or parking services on dates. Secure SIGN

Figure 7-1: Utah Utes Airtable database

The database can be updated, expanded, and refined at any time. One of the benefits of using an online database is that everyone has access to the most current version.

Once you have entered your projects and tasks, the power of the database takes over. You can ask questions and get answers with the click of a button. And you can ask virtually any question you can think of. For example, you could ask:

- What are all the tasks we must do in August?
- What parts of recruiting will our new assistant be doing?

- What is the full list of tasks for our director of operations?
- Who is involved in player development and how is the work being divided?
- Who is involved in making team travel arrangements?
- Which hotels have we stayed at in the past, who are our contacts, and what are their contact details?

Using your database, you could have printouts answering all of the above questions in less than five minutes.

LETTING STAFF GO

There will be times when a staff member doesn't work out. Perhaps they were not delivering the work required of their position. Maybe they didn't fit the culture. They may have had personality clashes with others. Their work ethic might not have been what was expected or needed. It could be that they refused to support the vision of the program. Or, there could have been inappropriate interactions between that person and other staff members or players.

When it is time to let someone go, you need to be sensitive to their feelings, but clear, direct, and unemotional in the act itself. Remember that you are letting the person go because their efforts were not moving the program forward, not because they failed as a human being. Unless there was unethical or inappropriate behavior, finding a graceful way for them to exit is good both for them and for your program. On the other hand, you never want to unload an unethical person on another program just to get rid of them quietly.

Jay Debertin, CEO of CHS, told us how he handles letting employees go:

"I just say 'this isn't going to work.' They may not have been ready for it, but most of the time they knew it was coming. If it did come as a shock to the employee, I would ask their leader: 'How could it be that you didn't talk about this with the employee?'"

Before you meet with a staff member, you must be clear in your own mind whether you have already decided to let them go or if you are still in the process of deciding. In givens terms, this is the difference between:

- I am letting you go. Here, the period shows the decision has already been made and it is a given you are letting them go.
- I am letting you go? Here, the question mark shows you are wavering in your decision, and it is not yet a given they will be let go.

If you end with a period, that means you have already decided to let the person go and this is a conversation to communicate your decision, not to discuss changing it. If you end with a question mark, that is telling the person that you haven't really decided and they can plead with you and perhaps talk you out of it. This will not serve either of your interests. If you are still at the question mark stage, you should be giving clear and direct feedback in the hope they improve. If you are at the period stage, they have already proven that they are unable to improve, and it is time for them to move on.

Depending on how the termination was done and how the person reacted, litigation is always a possibility. It is a wise idea to protect yourself by retaining texts and emails that support your decision to let the person go. If you sense litigation may be coming, having written formal reviews documenting the issues will help your case. This is a good practice to do with player meetings as well.

Once you have let the person go, it is time to reflect on what led to the termination and to diagnose how things got to that point. It might have been inevitable, but if perhaps you had done things differently, letting them go could have been avoided.

SUCCESSION PLANNING

One of the biggest differences in how athletics and business approach a topic is succession planning—the approach human resource departments in businesses use to identify and develop the next generation of leaders. The idea is that the current occupants of key positions will eventually retire or get promoted and their spots will need to be filled by candidates who have been prepared to take over. Rather than start the search for qualified candidates once someone leaves, succession planning begins years earlier to prepare the next occupant of that position to smoothly take over.

Businesses can create the organization chart for three years in the future because every key job has a backup that is being groomed to take over. The people being prepared to take over know they will get the job, and they have the time to grow their skills and experience to prepare for the promotion lying ahead of them. There are times when companies hire from the outside, but usually that is because their succession plan has shown them they do not have a qualified internal candidate to fill the vacant role.

In athletics, the approach is very different. Rather than having internal candidates to promote to the next level, the process typically begins with an external search once it is clear someone is about to leave. An assistant in the program may have a chance at the head coach position, but they normally will have to interview against candidates from a national search.

You could argue that because athletics programs are relatively small organizations (less than 30 people total), they don't have the need or the capability to do succession planning. But virtually all companies of that size have at least the beginnings of a succession plan, so it is not obvious why it wouldn't work in the world of sports. This is not to say you should spend a lot of time creating a detailed succession plan. But it does say that looking inside your own program for successors might be a valid and beneficial approach.

Nebraska volleyball used succession planning for their head coach position when the job was transferred from Terry Pettit to John Cook. Pettit recruited Cook and they overlapped for a season. This allowed Pettit to mentor Cook and prepare him for a smooth transition the following year when Pettit retired and Cook took the reins. Pettit told us:

> "Every coach in the country should have mentoring. Same as a president or a CEO."

Many programs have promoted an experienced assistant coach to the title of associate head coach. This could be useful for succession planning if the idea was to promote the associate head coach to head coach after an agreed upon number of years. But that does not normally happen. It usually does help the person get a head coaching position at another program, however.

USING YOUR NETWORK TO HELP
YOUR STAFF GET THEIR NEXT JOB

The conversations which lead to an assistant knowing they are ready for the next level job are never easy. Either they will think they are ready when you believe they are not, or you will see they are ready but they are not yet confident enough to take the next step. It is the head coach's job to prepare their people for the next level by giving them challenging tasks, honest and direct feedback, and by using the network they have built over the years to make the connections their people need.

Beth currently has multiple former assistants coaching at schools around the country. With her longevity, success, and credibility, coaches often call her for references, but her number one priority is to help her own staff first. This helps Beth land talented assistant coaches since they know she, with her massive amount of contacts, will help them when they are ready to move on.

Helping assistants and staff members get a head coaching position (or any other position they might be interested in) is an important part of Beth's philosophy. Athletics is a tight family, and networking is the way people find jobs. A good word to the right person could open up opportunities for a staff member that they could not create on their own. And since Beth has developed strong credibility with her peers over the years, they know she will not give a strong recommendation in order to get rid of a weak staff member.

You probably don't have the professional network that Beth has amassed during her thirty years in the profession. But, then again, neither did she when she started out. Beth made a conscious effort to meet people and get to know them so well that they became both her colleagues and her long-time friends.

The best advice we can give you on how to introduce yourself to people you don't know comes from Judy Robinett, the author of *How to Be a Power Connector*. In her book, she says:

> "Your best friend, first crush, spouse, mentor, co-worker, or teammate were strangers when you first met them. Whenever you think about networking, imagine that the next person you meet might turn out to be one of your closest friends."

MAIN POINTS IN THIS CHAPTER

- Professionalism needs to be taught.
- Staff norms define the ground rules for how to work in your program.
- Case study interviews enable you to see how an applicant thinks.
- Being designed to win requires that you hire the best people, not just those who look, act, and think like you do.
- Developing an easily accessible knowledge storehouse helps you bring new people up to speed more quickly than starting from scratch. This is critical in the high turnover world of athletics.
- When you let staff go, it is a judgment based on their performance, not on who they are as a person.
- Your network is a powerful tool to help you and your staff obtain their next jobs.

CHAPTER 8: RECRUITING AND DEVELOPING YOUR PLAYERS

"Put six random people on the court and they can compete hard, but they might not win. Being designed to win is deeper than the X's and the O's of the sport."

Dan Corotan (University of Utah volleyball assistant coach)

We will begin by discussing how to assemble your team. Then we will describe how to develop your individual players to their fullest potential. Finally, we will discuss how to meld your players into a winning team.

THE LIFE OF A STUDENT-ATHLETE IS A UNIQUE EXPERIENCE

The life of a collegiate athlete is filled with hard work, thrilling victories, and agonizing defeats. This level of competitiveness is happening while the athletes are full-time students who are living on their own for the first time. Beth tells her athletes:

"The four or five years you will spend as a college athlete is a unique experience you will never be able to relive. You will never have another experience like this because you can't get it in any other facet of your life."

Student-athletes pull together to achieve challenging goals. The amount of teamwork required is enormous, and the intensity unparalleled. Being a student-athlete teaches young people important lessons about life including understanding the value of good time management, how to work closely with others in a competitive arena, what it takes to be a leader, how to resolve conflicts, and how to communicate effectively. They will be members of other teams during the course of their lives, but nothing will compare to the intensity and pressure of performing in front of thousands of people who are judging the quality of their work in real time.

The NCAA limits the time allowed for collegiate athletes' sport to 20 hours a week. In reality, however, they put in closer to 30 to 40 hours a week when you add in time for preparation, rehab, and related activities such as travel, marketing appearances, and hosting recruits. When you add in their academic course load, the discipline and prioritizing required to keep all the plates spinning is incredible. Smart and successful coaches understand and respect the time demands of their players.

FILLING YOUR TALENT PIPELINE

The first step in recruiting is to understand your talent pipeline. It starts with players you are aware of that are potentially good enough to play at your level. You then narrow that list down to players you want to actively engage with, before further narrowing it down to the players to whom you want to make scholarship or walk-on offers. The last step is closing the deal with those you have offered.

The pipeline looks like this:

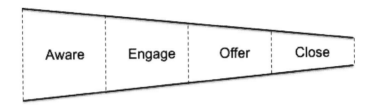

Figure 8-1: Recruitment pipeline

Each step can be expanded more fully:

- Aware (approximately 100 to 200 players per recruiting season).

  ° Attend high school matches and club tournaments.
  ° Speak with coaches and club directors.
  ° Network with fellow coaches and with both current and former players.
  ° Contact international colleagues and recruiting services.
  ° View videos submitted by interested players.
  ° Review prep athletes by rankings and accomplishments.

- Engage (approximately 30 players). Narrow the list by:

  ° Rating the current ability and/or eventual potential.
  ° Inviting them to camps and clinics on your campus and observing them firsthand.
  ° Evaluating their fit with your program.

◦ Estimating the likelihood they would be interested in your program. It is at this point you notify the player or their high school or club coach (depending on their age) of your interest. From there, you build a relationship with the coach, the player, and/or the player's family (once again, depending on the recruit's age).

◦ Eliminating players that are not interested in your program. Too many programs spend far too much time on this group.

- Offer (Usually 1 to 4 players)

  ◦ Call the recruit with the offer and send them the offer letter when NCAA rules allow it. Spend time with the recruit on your campus in an unofficial or official visit.

  ◦ Do a home visit (depending on their age).

- Close

  ◦ Spend time on the phone with the recruit as decision time nears.

  ◦ Meet with the player and the player's family.

  ◦ Invite the player and their family up to campus as much as possible to watch matches and practices.

  ◦ Continue to deepen your relationship with all parties.

  ◦ Understand the player's objectives and identify how your program would meet them.

  ◦ Help the recruit see that what your school offers is the right fit for them.

  ◦ Secure a verbal commitment.

  ◦ Obtain the player's signature on a National Letter of Intent.

USING GIVENS TO NARROW YOUR RECRUITING PIPELINE

As you move from Aware to Engage to Offer to Close on your pipeline, you and your recruiting coordinator will make judgements about the current capabilities and potentials of numerous athletes, many of whom you will have only seen on video. To help you with this process of narrowing down athletes, you can employ a set of givens about what you are looking for at each position.

Here are examples of givens by position:

- Outside Hitters

  - If they are on the low end of jump height, they must possess above average passing skills.
  - The higher the player plays above the net, the more willing we will be to look at a player with less developed passing skills.
  - The player's arm swing mechanics must not have any major technical issues.
  - They must possess a well-rounded skill set.

- Middle Blockers

  - They need to have a "workhorse" mentality.
  - They must have either great size or possess great quickness. Should they have both, that is an obvious plus.
  - They must play high above the net.
  - They need to move well laterally.

- Setters

  ○ They must have intangible qualities such as effective communication skills, strong leadership capabilities, and solid interpersonal skills.

  ○ A high level of athleticism is preferred. Athletic attributes could be quickness, size, or strength.

  ○ If athleticism is not in the top 10%, then their setting skill level must be high.

  ○ They need to have a high-level volleyball IQ and the ability to develop nuanced understandings of situations.

- Liberos

  ○ Passing is the most important skill in volleyball. This skill is the priority we look for in a libero.

  ○ A straight and simple platform is required with a natural feel for the passing skill.

  ○ A high level of athleticism is required.

  ○ Size is important. If they are smaller, they must still have great range on defense.

  ○ They must be competent in the skills of serving and setting.

Just the process of creating these givens will help you and your recruiting team visualize the quality of athletes for whom they should be searching. These positional givens will allow you to eliminate athletes who would not make your program better before you have invested a lot of time in them.

THE CRITICAL ROLE OF WALK-ONS

Programs have fewer scholarships than roster spots, and so some of your athletes will be walk-ons rather than being on scholarship. By inviting someone to walk on, the coach sends the message that the player is good enough to be on the team and would contribute to the program. The walk-on position is critical to the success of most NCAA sports teams, and the arrangement often makes sense for both the school and the player.

The advantage of a walk-on to the school is obvious in that they have a player on the roster who is skilled enough to contribute but who is not costing a scholarship. Walking on can be quite attractive for the recruit as well. It enables them to get the full college athletic experience at a school they may have wanted to attend for academic reasons. In addition, they may be able to get a scholarship later in their career if they earn playing time and a scholarship becomes available.

THE UNDERAPPRECIATED VALUE OF HOLDING BACK SCHOLARSHIPS

Depending on your sport, you may have the flexibility of offering partial scholarships. However, for many sports, scholarships are head count full rides that cannot be split up, last for multiple years, and are hard to change once awarded.

The value of scholarships you hold back for late developing high school players, international players, graduate transfers, transfers from junior colleges, or transfers from other four-year universities has become greater since the transfer portal has been in place. In the past, you might have awarded all of your scholarships without giving it a second thought. Now you might regret tying up a scholarship on a mid-level player when you could have held it back for a more talented player to be named later. If you haven't held back a scholarship, you may lose a great player unless they have a burning desire to join your program and sufficient family funds to make it happen.

This approach is a balancing act between a bird in the hand today and an unknown future possibility that might have a large upside. When Utah had a great year and was ranked as a top-10 program, several high-level international players and transfers expressed their interest in joining the program. Retaining a scholarship for these athletes could provide a substantial upgrade by filling a particular need with an experienced and talented player.

WHEN PLAYERS LEAVE YOUR PROGRAM

There are many reasons a player might leave your program, including:

- Stronger players may leave because they believe they can join a higher-ranked program or one with a stronger commitment to winning than their current program. They may feel they are better than their current school.
- Weaker players may leave because they are buried in the depth chart and do not expect to see playing time. That same player might be a starter at a different program.
- Players may leave due to disagreements over the coaching style, the style of play, their role on the team, and/or hurt feelings between staff or teammates.
- Players may leave because they dislike the school, location, culture, or weather. This may also tie into family or relationship issues.

When a player leaves, it is often a win for the player and the program. The player may find a better fit elsewhere, and, given the issues that caused the player to leave, they were unlikely to have contributed to the team's success had they stayed. Even a strong player might have dragged the team down if they had stayed but continuously displayed a negative attitude.

There are times when a player leaves without sufficient warning to make a backup plan. It is difficult for players to be open about leaving and their reasons for doing so, and they can take the easy way out and just let the staff know after they have already entered the transfer portal. Talking about leaving is a hard thing to do, but like most difficult conversations, it is better to have it than not.

There are times when the push for a player to leave comes from the staff rather than the player. There are NCAA restrictions about pulling scholarships and doing so would break a promise the program made to the athlete. But there should never be an issue with the staff having an honest talk with a player and letting them know their future at the program might not include much playing time. Should the player choose to stay, they do so with full knowledge of how the staff sees their future and with the understanding that their opportunities may be limited.

DEVELOPING THE COMPLETE PLAYER

Utah takes a holistic approach to a student-athlete's experience during their four years as a collegiate athlete. Besides physical training, their growth and development includes academics, leadership, nutrition, mental health, goal setting, communication skills, conflict management abilities, and career preparedness, to name just a few.

This development does not happen by chance. At Utah, the coaches and staff intentionally and systematically provide opportunities to teach lifelong lessons and to teach the love of being a lifelong learner. For example, when a conflict arises between two players or a between a coach and a player, the easiest thing to do would be to ignore it, but the growth opportunity lies in addressing the issue and having the series of uncomfortable conversations that will lead to resolution of the conflict. Teaching players and staff conflict resolutions skills gives them tools they can use to work through every situation, both on court and off.

John Dunning, American Volleyball Coaches Association Hall of Famer, describes his style for dealing with conflicts in this way:

> "I use matter-of-fact communication skills. You have to listen, and I want to figure it out in a non-emotional way."

Another example of holistic player development is the DISC Behavioral Profile program, which Beth uses with her players as well as her staff. Teaching players about different behavioral styles helps them to understand the differences between themselves and the people they may have thought they knew. By learning about these differences, players learn how to better relate to their teammates and coaches and develop healthy working relationships to achieve challenging goals. Incorporating DISC or another tool that provides insights into differences and behaviors will help your players learn lessons that will benefit them long after they finish their time on the field, gym, or the court.

DEFINING MEANINGFUL ROLES FOR EVERY PLAYER

Defining truly meaningful roles for every player is critical to developing a high-performing team. Ensuring that players thoroughly understand and accept their roles through clear and repeated communication is critical. When a player's role is well defined, the team will thrive with every player contributing from their assigned seat on the bus.

Defining the roles of bench players is particularly challenging. Your bench players were most likely stars on their high school or club teams, and almost assuredly expected to remain stars within your program. Helping them accept and take pride in their role as a bench player means dealing with their egos and helping them see they that they will still be contributing to the program's success.

It is important for coaches and teammates to understand that each role comes with its own specific challenges. The last players on the bench have the difficult role of supporting those in the game, meet, or match, even though they themselves will seldom see playing time despite having put in the same amount of work. The star player's role is difficult in that they carry the majority of the pressure for team success and cannot look to someone else to lighten their load. Both roles are critical, both are hard, both have value, and both need to be positively reinforced again and again.

That does not mean a player's role is static and won't change over the course of a year as a player improves or regresses, or as injuries affect the depth chart. Any change in roles should be explicitly discussed so that everyone is on the same page. Stealth role changes don't work.

THE IMPORTANCE OF PLAYER LEADERSHIP

Leadership matters for players just as it does for staff. It is an intangible that is hard to measure, but it's easy to see when it is lacking. Normally, leadership will come from the better players and those in upper classes, but this will not always be the case. A leader may show themselves in their first year even before receiving significant playing time. Their sphere of influence will expand as they gain respect from other players.

Being a servant leader (as opposed to a command and control leader) is the most effective style of leadership in athletics. Great leaders understand what the team needs and are constantly seeking ways to help individual players contribute. If a player is struggling with a standard, a servant leader will step in and help that player find a way to address their issues.

Leaders may not always be the most liked, but that is not their job. Their job is to use their positions of influence in a supportive way to help the team achieve their goals. Leading is not yelling from the front, it is listening and supporting others to help them carry out their roles for the good of the team.

Beth has gone away from naming team captains over the past few years. Instead, she has created a leadership council composed of juniors and seniors to bring a broader and more diverse set of ideas and views than she would get from one or two captains. Coaches meet regularly with the leadership council, and the council meets on its own as well. The council approach provides more opportunities to lead than naming captains does, and ensures that no experienced player can hide behind the leadership of others.

DEALING WITH DISCIPLINARY ISSUES

When staff or players wander outside the circle of trust or go beyond the standards set for the team, it raises questions. How do you deal with the individual? Is there one standard for all? Is it a team issue or an individual issue? Should you let it slide or come down hard?

Coaching is a business of dealing with people. There are many grey areas, and treating all players the same doesn't necessarily mean fairness. Each player is unique and motivated by different things. Getting players to understand the need for standards and consequences is important. However, so is judgment about the specific behaviors and personalities of the individuals involved.

Issues naturally arise when you have highly competitive people working closely together in a pressure-filled, competitive environment. Sometimes these issues need to be addressed with the entire team, sometimes individually, and sometimes both are required. These conversations are private and should not be shared with others outside of the team.

An example of this occurred when the team was playing in the hometown of one of the players. During this trip, that player had not been respectful with a teammate. Some coaches would have chosen to sit the offending player, but since it was in the player's hometown, this action would have sent a loud and public message to the fans and her family that there was a problem within the team.

Beth chose to handle it internally, both with the involved players and with the entire team since the problem was well known inside the locker room. Beth required the player who had been disrespectful to apologize to her targeted teammate as well as to the entire team for the disruption she had caused.

Beth decided not to hurt the team to make a point to the player, but this decision was contentious within the coaching staff since the assistants were pushing for the player to be benched. Although the coaching staff did not agree with what Beth had decided, they presented a unified front to the team to support the decision.

The above example led to a teachable moment using the DISC model. I's and S's are motivated by relationships and may have been satisfied with the apology knowing the relationship was being mended. The D's are much more motivated by results and the same apology would be seen as getting the distraction out of the way so the team could get back to winning. The C's would have been satisfied because a fair process had been employed. The consequences for the player were seen as sufficient by the team, but for very different reasons based on their DISC behavioral styles.

MEASURING INDIVIDUALS' CONTRIBUTION TO THE TEAM

Team development mandates putting the best team on the court, not just the best players. Measuring player performance through statistics is one way of understanding who the best players are and who should be on the court the most. Statistics, however, are not the only way to determine whether a player is the best fit for the team. Sometimes players that are not the best statistically can be the most valuable contributors.

There are players who make the others around them better or who play a supportive role that fits well with other players on the court. A good example in volleyball is a six-rotation outside hitter who is a great passer but only an average attacker. That player might be more valuable than an attacker who has a higher kill percentage but cannot pass. If an attacker is an average or below-average passer, it is harder to set to the middle attacker. Setting the middle is necessary to spread out the offense and makes it more difficult for the opponent to defend a system with multiple attackers coming at them. A great passer makes the team better even if they are not the primary scorer.

The Utah volleyball team uses a set of measurements they call vital stats. They believe these metrics have a high correlation with winning, and they are the standards by which the coaches measure team and individual progress in a given area. Malia Shoji, University of Utah volleyball associate head coach, told us this:

> "You need to measure progress towards your goals with vital stats. For example, you might find that the top 10% of the teams perform at a certain level in the side-out game. But right now, our team is not performing at this level and needs to step it up."

DEVELOPING ANNUAL GOALS ALIGNED WITH THE PROGRAM VISION

At the forefront of team dynamics is making sure everyone in the program has bought into the vision. While the Utah volleyball program has a clear and concise vision that the players learn about during the recruiting process, it does not stop there. Once they join the team, they spend hours and hours developing annual goals aligned with the overall vision.

Developing these annual goals starts as a brainstorming session with the coaches and the team leaders. The remaining players join in after a rough first draft is created. This collaborative work results in a thoughtful plan that has clear objectives and standards, and that fits within the overall program vision. Engaging with the entire team is essential to make sure all ideas are raised and everyone's voice is heard.

The conversations leading up to the annual goals are where the bulk of the value lies. Each member of the team feels listened to and takes pride in having contributed to the creation of the goals. Their understanding and ownership are powerful and contribute directly to achieving the desired results.

Patti Tibaldi, NAIA women's basketball Hall of Famer, emphasized the importance of this when she said:

"You must have a consistency of vision that is shared by staff and players."

THE CONTRACT WITH PARENTS

This adherence to the team vision extends to the parents of the players as well. Beth has a contract for parents to sign listing the appropriate parental behaviors, which lets them know what actions she believes are and are not consistent with the program's values and what behaviors would best support their child. It also states how the Utah volleyball program will treat their child. Fair, respectful, honest, and caring are just a few qualities a parent can expect from the coaching staff.

Being supportive of both the coaching staff and their child and leaving the coaching to the coaches is what the staff asks of the parents. This is not a binding contract, just an understanding between parents and their child's coach that explicitly defines how each should support the young athlete.

TEAM BONDING

Creating bonding opportunities to get to know each other as people rather than just as players and coaches is powerful. Knowing someone's background, family, and the community they were raised in helps everyone understand the different lenses people use to see the world.

While getting to know each other on a deeper personal basis is essential, simply hanging out is not an efficient or effective way to achieve this goal. Instead, Beth creates more impactful social and interactive opportunities for the team during down time. She often tells the team:

> "Even though there are great friendships in our group, we are not a social group. We are not together in this locker room because we are all friends. We are together because we are a group of individuals trying to form a team to compete at a very high level."

Activities such as having lunch with a teammate with five questions designed to get to better know each other, or a buddy or mentor system to learn how to best support each other, are helpful for improving team dynamics. Also, fun activities such as escape rooms and game nights at hotels are great ways to interact and learn about each other in different settings.

Players share a room with different teammates on each trip. They also sit next to the person they are rooming with on the bus and at meals. Proximity is the key to communication, and by matching different players on each road trip, everyone gets to know each other on a one-on-one basis.

Every player has a "sphere of influence" that affects those around them either positively or negatively. This is why decisions on locker assignments and travel roommates are such key issues. A team that spends quality time together knows how everyone thinks, and how they can help each other.

BUILDING TEAM MORALE

Team morale needs to be monitored and addressed continuously. Doing so requires open and honest communication between the coaching staff and the captain or team leaders, or any individual player that is willing to share. Players need to know that you will not shoot the messenger if they bring you bad news. And you need to listen to understand, even if you disagree with what you are hearing.

It is important not to react to everything shared with you. Instead, look and listen for trends that may be helping or hurting the team. Blowing your top when you hear things you did not know will not lead to more openness in the future.

NOT ALL SKILLS CONTRIBUTE EQUALLY TO WINNING

Programs are better at developing certain skills than others. This may be because of a coach's passion for that position, it may be the position they themselves played, or perhaps the coach just has experience and feels comfortable coaching that position. For example, Utah has always been considered a very good blocking team. This was true in the 90s and it is still true today.

Understanding what correlates with winning and losing makes you a better coach. Spending time on aspects of the game that do not correlate strongly with winning is not a good use of your time. You may improve in this area, but even if you succeed in doing so, it is unlikely to result in additional wins. Beth is still passionate about the blocking game, but data show that passing and attacking are the two most productive skills in volleyball and that serving is one of the most important skills because it disrupts passing and attacking.

While Utah is still a great blocking team, Beth spends less time on that skill so she can invest more time training passing, attacking, and serving. Because of this, Utah has been ranked one of the top three Pac-12 passing and offensive teams of the last few years, and these skills have turned directly into additional wins.

TOOL: THE UTAH RED CHART

Management consultants create charts that visualize many different attributes on a single page. Using this approach, we created the Utah RED chart. This chart enables you to see at a glance snapshots of your current players by position and class, the rate of improvement of each player, the ceiling you anticipate for each player, and the gaps you must fill to be successful.

RED stands for Recruiting, Effort, and Development. Recruiting describes a player's talent on the day they arrive at your program. Effort describes their desire to improve and their work ethic. Development describes their growth mindset, improvement path, and how close they are to reaching their ceiling.

Beth used this chart with Berkeley Oblad when Oblad was deciding whether or not to return for her fifth-year senior season after having sat out the year before recovering from elbow surgery. The insight arising from the tool was that Utah was wonderfully positioned to have a great season but had one roster weakness. Utah had AVCA All-Americans at outside hitter, opposite, and setter. The Utes also had a great libero who ended up setting the program's career dig record. The only position that was lacking in experience was Oblad's position at middle blocker. Oblad had been an honorable mention AVCA All-American the year before her elbow injury, and she was the perfect piece to complete the puzzle.

The Utah RED chart enabled Oblad to see how the team would look with her returning and how well positioned it would be to do something the program had never done before. She chose to come back, greatly helped the team, and improved her professional opportunities by earning AVCA Second-Team All-American honors. Those honors helped her begin her professional career in Hungary and now in France.

This was the first use of the Utah RED chart, and even if it never helped with anything again, it still would have been worth developing just for this one decision. Fortunately, however, the chart can be updated and used again and again for enhancing recruitment, player development, and team development.

PLOTTING YOUR UTAH RED CHART

You can download a blank Utah RED PowerPoint slide for your own use from www.leohopf.com or www.bethlauniere.com. Trust us that it is much easier to start with a pre-made template than to build your own from scratch.

The chart begins with the following:

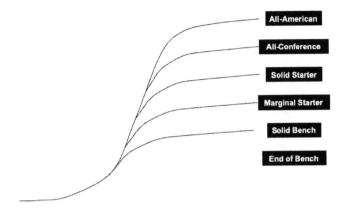

Figure 8-2: Utah RED Chart: starting point

The higher a player is vertically on the chart, the greater their current level of play.

Step two is to add the rate of improvement on the bottom of the chart:

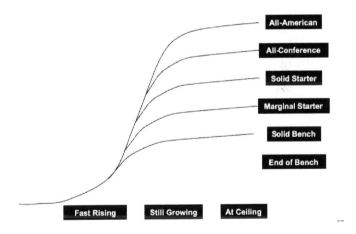

Figure 8-3: Utah RED Chart: adding growth rate

The farther to the right a player is, the closer they are to being as good as they will ever be. The farther to the left a player is, the faster they are growing.

Now that the axes on the chart are set, you can plot players on the chart and interpret what their position on it means.

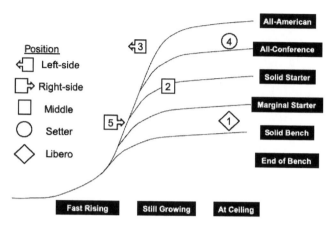

Figure 8-4: Utah RED Chart: plotting players

The easiest way to mark which player is which is to use a shape for their position and place their jersey number inside the shape. You can also color code the shapes to show how many years of eligibility each player has remaining.

In the example above, player #1 is a libero who is a solid bench player and may have reached their ceiling. Player #2 is a solid starter at middle blocker and is still growing. They may very well be on their way to being named to the All-Conference team or to even higher honors. Player #3 is a left-side hitter and a clear star. They are already near All-American level and are still improving rapidly. They are on the path for consideration as the national Player of the Year. Player #4 is a setter, has reached the All-Conference level, and that is as far as they might ever go. Player #5 is a right-side hitter who is just getting ready to start but is improving rapidly.

The Utah RED tool is easily adaptable to other sports. Football might use one chart for each of their positions since plotting the entire team would make the chart too crowded. Gymnastics would replace the volleyball positions with their four rotations of vault, bars, beam, and floor exercise. Swimming and track would replace the volleyball positions with their various events.

DEVELOPING INSIGHTS USING THE UTAH RED CHART

Here is a completed Utah RED chart showing an entire volleyball roster. (This is an example only, not the plotting of an actual team. We will use the pronoun 'they' in this example since the tool works equally well for any gender.)

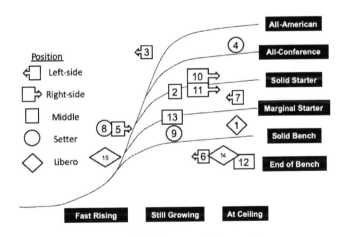

Figure 8-5: Utah RED Chart: completed example

Now that you have the entire roster plotted, you can analyze the Utah RED chart and see what it is trying to tell you. The above chart might raise the following issues for individual players:

- Our star player (#3) might get frustrated because they are above the other players and still improving quickly. As the gap grows, this player may feel that the others are not pulling their weight.
- We are weak at backup setter. We will need to give our 2nd setter plenty of reps in practice so they are ready to go if needed. Player #8 is improving, but they are not ready yet. And since #4 is injury prone, we are at risk at this position.
- We are weak at libero. Are there any other players who could switch to that position?
- Player #12 was highly recruited and has a full scholarship. It is now clear, however, that they might never contribute to the team and they have been the source of increasing drama that is causing resentment and distractions. What actions should we take?
- Our middle blockers are solid but not great. Is there a transfer or international player we could pick up to strengthen the position?
- Might players #6, #12, and #14 begin to stir up unrest as they feel they are not getting the playing time they expected?
- Player #3 is a junior, and we have no left-side hitters on the way up to take their place when they graduate. How will the offense need to be adjusted when #7 takes over?
- Player #9's improvement has slowed dramatically this year. Why did this happen, and what can we do to get them growing again?

The chart also raises questions about the overall program:

- When you consider the upcoming graduations, what should our recruiting targets be?
- Are we doing all we can to develop our players, or are

they moving too quickly to the right on the chart and reaching their ceilings too soon?

- Which positions are we strong at developing, and which positions are more difficult for us to improve?
- When you look at the chart as a whole, are our players at the level required to win in our conference?

Players on different parts of the chart have different contributions to make to a winning team. You need balance between those delivering today's success and those building tomorrow's.

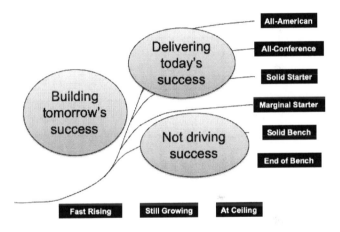

Figure 8-6: Utah RED Chart: contributions to the team's success

The players on the left are growing fast and will be your players of the future. The ones on the top are doing the heavy lifting to deliver today's success. The players on the lower right are not driving success but may be contributing through their impact on culture and by helping the other players develop. They may also be a net negative if their focus is on their lack of glory and minimal playing time.

PLOTTING YOUR PLAYERS ON
THE UTAH RED CHART

You plot your players both up and down (their current level of play) and left and right (their rate of improvement). To do so, you need to make judgements on a player-by-player basis.

To plot the up/down, you can use both external and internal measurements. These include:

External:

- All-American, All-Region, and All-Conference selections.
- Conference and national "Player of the Week" awards.
- Preseason honors watch lists.
- Preseason all-tournament teams and MVP awards.
- Statistical comparisons with other players at the same position in your conference, your region, and nationwide.
- Validation from opposing coaches.

Internal:

- Judgments by your coaching staff on if they are making changes and have a growth mindset.

Plotting the left/right positions also has some external benchmarks but is primarily based on the internal judgements of your staff.

External

- Benchmarking with comparable players in different programs.

Internal

- Judgment by your coaching staff on if they are making changes and have a growth mindset

- Rate of statistical improvement from year to year.

There is one thing you should be careful with once you have created your chart, and that is letting too many people see it. First, that would provide opponents with a huge head start in scouting your program. Second, and more importantly, if you have a player on the right side of the chart, it means you believe their rate of improvement has slowed. Should the player see that, it might become a self-fulfilling prophecy.

If you are doubting their ability to improve, their dedication to getting better might weaken. And, after all, you might be wrong in thinking they had reached their potential. You would hate for them to give up rather than to continue to work hard and perhaps surprise you with their growth.

MAIN POINTS IN THIS CHAPTER

- You need to manage your talent pipeline.
- Establishing positional givens enables you to quickly screen out players who will not succeed in your program.
- Programs which are designed to win maximize both player and team goals and development.
- All players need to have meaningful roles that enable them to contribute to the overall success of the team.
- The Utah RED Chart allows you to visualize your entire program at a glance.

CHAPTER 9: DEVELOPING FANS AND DONORS

"One word—SMILES. This team has fun. I can see a difference from other programs while I am sitting courtside. This is a group that, from the head coach on down to the support staff and players, loves volleyball."

Russ Swonson (Utah's volleyball announcer)

A committed and passionate fan base is fundamental to any program designed to win. It is part of a coach's responsibility to increase attendance whether by themselves or in conjunction with their marketing department. Having great attendance is vital to Beth's vision of winning at the highest level.

Fans energize the team and are major contributors to home court advantage. Fan participation, when properly cultivated, can become a virtuous circle for team growth. More fans lead to a better environment, which leads to more successful recruiting, which leads to more success, which leads to more fans. Fans (particularly younger fans who are junior players) remind the athletes of when they were the ones waiting in line for autographs and provide them with perspective on their impact as role models.

CONNECTING WITH FANS

Fans attend matches hoping to see their team emerge victorious, and nothing builds a fan base like winning. But most fans quickly learn to enjoy the experience of the game and their attachment to the players, regardless of the outcome.

The most successful programs focus on the fan experiences and keep entertaining their fans even during breaks in the action. They build linkages with players and the program through:

- Inviting young fans to line up along the sideline and high-five the starters as they are introduced.
- Post-match autograph sessions.
- Videos about the players shared on the video board during matches. These same videos can also be shared on social media.
- Fan buses to nearby road games.
- Theme nights with costume contests and matching music. Harry Potter, Star Wars, and Frozen theme nights are always popular.
- Partnerships with local elementary schools to host a "Future Scholars" event during a preseason midday match.
- Skills contests with fans as participants during breaks in the action.
- Youth on-court scrimmages at halftime or between sets.
- Summer camps led by staff and players. These both delight the attendees and teach players about the

importance of mentoring and inspiring the next generation.

One of the most effective recent additions at the University of Utah for building fan connection was to have the players stay on the floor and invite the fans onto the court for ten-minutes after each home match. Win or lose, the fans can take pictures with, and get autographs from, their favorite players.

It took five years to get permission to do this due to concerns about protecting the floor from street shoes. Once it began, however, fans deepened their relationships with the program by spending informal time with the players and coaches. The sight of a dozen young kids mobbing a player with shrieks of excitement brings joy to players, coaches, parents, and other fans.

VENUES AND FACILITIES

Crimson Court was a beloved little volleyball-only gym that had a storied past of big-time matches. It held approximately 1,500 fans packed like sardines with a raucous student section cheering passionately mere inches from opposing servers. The Utes won over 80% of their matches on this court while being ranked among the best volleyball programs in the country.

Figure 9-1: Crimson Court

There were huge wins that will forever be a part of the folklore of Crimson Court. There were numerous wins over BYU when both teams were ranked nationally and with fans overflowing the bleachers. Utah defeated Stanford when the Cardinal were ranked number one in the country and UCLA when the Bruins were ranked number six. In 2001, Utah emerged victorious over Utah State in the NCAA tournament to go to its first-ever Sweet 16. As Beth walked off the court, she made eye contact with the proud alumnae who had done so much to build the program. Crimson Court was where Beth won her 100th, 200th, 300th, and 400th career matches.

In 2008, the Utes beat Colorado State to win the Mountain West Conference Championship, after which Utah proceeded to cut down the volleyball net while the players, coaches, and fans sang and danced jubilantly to "We are the Champions." Beth's idea of cutting down the net as is done in basketball started an NCAA tradition for the volleyball national champions to cut down their nets and keep pieces of it for mementos.

As hard as it was to leave Crimson Court, the program made

the move to the 15,000 seat Huntsman Center just before their third Pac-12 season. Because of all of the other changes underway (see Chapter 2,) there was insufficient bandwidth to make the move during the first two seasons. Most of the other Pac-12 teams played in their university's main arenas, and Beth felt it was a critical move for the success of the program.

Figure 9-2: Volleyball at the Huntsman Center

The Huntsman Center had just been renovated with a state-of-the-art video board, new lighting and sound systems, and a quarter-million-dollar curtain to section off the top of the bowl to create a more fan-friendly environment with a 7,000-seat capacity. Attendance jumped by 500 fans per match as soon as the move to the Huntsman Center occurred. Utah now averages close to 3,000 volleyball fans and has turned a great basketball arena into a great volleyball arena.

The main reasons for the move were to give Utah volleyball instant credibility as a premier sport within the athletic department and with recruits, and to put it on the same level as men's and women's basketball and gymnastics in terms of facilities. Banners of volleyball players past and present will hang in the rafters of the storied Huntsman Center instead of in the small gym in the Health, Physical Education, and Recreation building in which Crimson Court was housed. And life-sized banners of each volleyball player now hang in the Huntsman Center concourse.

Figure 9-3: Utah volleyball's new locker room.

Recruits take notice not only of the Huntsman Center, but also of the numerous other athletic facilities being built or renovated within the Utah Athletic Department. A brand-new state-of-the-art locker room costing close to a half-million dollars is the new home for Utah volleyball players. They work out in the Sorenson Performance Center that was built in conjunction with the new thirty-million-dollar men's and women's basketball practice facility. Suddenly, the University of Utah had some of the best facilities in the Pac-12 and nationally.

The facilities upgrade created a completely new level of experience for the players, and the move to the Huntsman Center created a completely new level of experience for the fans.

THE BLOCK U BOOSTER CLUB

The Block U Club is Utah's volleyball booster club. It was redesigned two years ago (including replacing the outdated Spiker Club moniker) to be a more fan-centric club giving enhanced access to players and to inside information about the program.

As an example of one of the changes, at post-match Spiker Club pizza parties, players generally sat together with their families. Staff and players stood up and shared comments with the group, but personal interaction was limited. Rather than cementing relationships, it felt awkward for the fans who were invited but had the feeling they were outsiders. At the redesigned Block U events, players, their families, fans, and staff mingle freely, which makes the fans feel much more welcome.

Another addition to the club was better inside access to the finer points of the game. This past year, Beth invited the Block U Club members to an in-depth scouting session in the locker room. She shared the scouting report on the next day's opponent, showed video and explained what to look for, and presented the game plan to the club. This educated them and gave them the inside scoop on what to watch for in the match.

Membership in the Block U Club costs $100 and comes with a Block U T-shirt, three concession coupons, signed posters and team photos, and five general admission tickets to any match. But it is the fan experiences that accompany Block U Club membership that resonate with fans. Block U Club events include:

- Pre-match chalk-talks by the coaching staff describing the match plan and scouting report.

- Attendance at a practice to watch the staff and players from chairs on the floor and see firsthand the hard work the team puts in.
- Post-match dinners with staff, players, and their families. Players spread out across the tables, so fans get a chance to get to know them better.
- Emails from the program to update the club members on what is happening with the team and the players.

These events enable the members to learn more about the game and the players. It makes them feel special and that they are valued by the program.

THE NEED FOR DONORS

The Block U Club also fosters potential donors that every program needs. Most of a sport's operating budget (which may run into the hundreds of thousands or millions of dollars) is funded by ticket sales, large donations, student fees, and other university sources. Items in the budget typically include scholarships, salaries for coaches and staff, uniforms, equipment, recruiting expenses, travel expenses for road matches, etc. These big-ticket items make up the bulk of the program's expenditure, and are the must-haves to simply compete.

What is not typically included in the budget are the nice-to-haves. Budgets are tight, and they cover only what is necessary. Getting administrative approvals for optional expenditures ranges from challenging to near impossible.

Budgets can also be cut back suddenly and unexpectedly due to financial constraints. During the COVID-19 crisis, for example, many programs were required to take across-the-board cuts from previously approved amounts, and a spending freeze went into effect when all fall sports, including football, were postponed. If any of the nonessential, but helpful, extras that were cut from the budget were to be reinstated, it would have to be through the generosity of donors.

The amounts required for the nice-to-haves are orders of magnitude less than the costs to run the program. An extra $2,000 would not be noticed in the scholarship pool. But that amount would buy an experience or a tool that can't be justified as absolutely required, but which would help the players mentally or physically. It could buy an extra computer or camera, massages for the team during a tournament, or a day at a resort for the team. These small things can have big impacts on the team's attitude and performance.

THE DONOR PYRAMID

Fundraising has historically been viewed as a pyramid with a large number of small donors at the base and a small number of large donors at the top.

Figure 9-4: Donor pyramid

At the base are the fans who make up the largest group. Each fan is unlikely to give a large amount, but the cumulative donations from many fans can add up. The next levels are the occasional and annual donors who can be counted on for medium-sized contributions. Next come major donors, who, by definition, have deeper pockets and give larger amounts. At the top of the pyramid are those who commit to planned giving, usually as a result of a deep and long-lasting love of the program. Planned giving means their donations come from their estate after their passing. Due to the potentially large size of planned gifts, their donations may gain attention in the media and inspire others to give as well.

Development professionals create donor tables to set goals for a fundraising campaign. For example, they might target 100 donors to give $X, 10 donors to give $10X, and 1 donor to give $100X. If you multiply the number of donors at each level by the amount that level gives, you end up targeting roughly the same amount of money raised at each level of the pyramid.

ISSUES WITH THE DONOR PYRAMID

The traditional idea of the pyramid is that individuals would start at the bottom and work their way up towards higher levels of giving over time. Development professionals provide increasing perks and recognition as you go up the pyramid with the goal of enticing donors to rise to the next higher level.

The donor pyramid does not always work this way. Some people come out of nowhere and jump to the top. Other donors skip up and down the levels depending on their current level of interest and availability of funds.

The main challenge with the pyramid approach, however, is that it is university-centric rather than donor-centric. It sees fans as donor units and treats fundraising as a numbers game with large databases of phone numbers and email addresses. People who work in development normally have a list of institutional priorities they must promote rather than being open to what donors would like to support.

For coaches in particular, the university-centric approach may not make sense. Most of the time, a coach is not trying to raise money for a renovation running into the millions of dollars. That might happen once a decade and would generally be driven by the development office as one of a list of university priorities.

Every year, however, there are small things that could be contributed by a single donor. Examples might include new chairs for the locker room, a portable smart board for the practice court, or funds to bring a massage therapist along for NCAA tournament road matches. Most of the time coaches are not looking for hundreds of donors on a pyramid. They are looking for a small number of donors who are deeply engaged with the program and who would find pleasure in opportunities to help the team.

THE UTAH DONOR-CENTRIC MODEL

Beth follows a donor-centric model at Utah. Her pyramid looks like this:

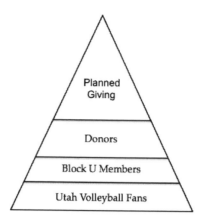

Figure 9-5: Beth's donor-centric pyramid

The fans support the program financially through ticket sales. The Block U members are season ticket holders and they pay an additional $100 to belong to the Block U Club. These two groups are handled chiefly by marketing and other staff. Most of Beth's time is spent at the donor level, working with a small number of contributors that Beth knows personally and interacts with regularly.

Beth listens to these donors and learns their specific interests so she can help them identify opportunities that would resonate with them and make them excited to give. Rather than pushing a funding need onto the donors, she allows them to pull ideas from her and make decisions on their own.

For example, a business professional dealing with large amounts of data in their job might find it enjoyable to give money for a graduate student to enhance the statistics collection and analysis for the program. By following this approach, donors are not asked to give money for some undefined investment. Instead, when they give, they do so because their money is being used for something that is meaningful for them.

Beth keeps a running list of "nice-to-haves" that might interest her donors, each at a suggested price point. This gives the donors an idea of the type of things they could support, and it enables them to talk with Beth about the things that interest them the most.

INVOLVE YOUR DONORS AND LET THEM TAILOR THEIR GIFTS

The price points should always be flexible to enable a donor to participate in defining the donation. For example, a few years ago, Beth needed to replace the chairs in the locker room. She added chairs to her "nice-to-haves" list and attached a price tag that would allow her to replace the worn-out director's chairs with new chairs of the same style.

One of the donors saw the chairs on her list and asked Beth to provide details of what made for a good locker room chair. In the ensuing discussion, the drawbacks of the current chairs came out: they were somewhat flimsy and unstable, they were not on wheels and so were difficult to rearrange, and they didn't give the locker room a touch of class.

Rather than simply replicating the current chairs, the donor asked Beth to get details on the chairs in the football locker room. The donor then asked Beth to order the next level up, so that volleyball would have the best chairs on campus. The dollar amount of the gift was much higher than Beth had originally requested, but the new rolling chairs were a big upgrade for the locker room and the donor had the satisfaction of influencing the gift. As a perk, the donor received two of the Utah branded chairs for their own home, providing a constant reminder of their bond with the program.

It is important that donors receive feedback on the impact of their gifts. This might come from thank you notes, social media postings, or special opportunities to meet with the team. For example, one of Utah's donor families hosts the spring volleyball awards banquet at their home. The tie this creates with the team is unparalleled. For the donor, they get to look forward to the event all year. For the players, it's a fun team-building event and an opportunity to connect with community members who can serve as role models and resources.

It pays to think creatively about ways to welcome donors into your program. They are giving money because they appreciate your team and it makes them happy to support it. You are letting them inside the tent, and once in, they will want to stay in.

ASKING DONORS FOR MONEY

There is often a disconnect in that coaches may be hesitant to ask for money even when donors would be happy to give it. Coaches may not want to offend a fan by asking for more than just the price of their ticket to support the program. Asking for money is uncomfortable for most people, and fundraising is not a major part of the training for becoming a coach.

Hesitancy to ask potential donors for money can place your program at a competitive disadvantage. Institutional fundraisers can't build the kind of connections with potential donors that a coach can develop. If all you can afford is the bare minimum provided by your university to physically appear at your home and road matches, your staff and players will become jealous of programs offering extras that you cannot.

In addition, you will be missing out on the chance to build stronger and more rewarding bonds with those who love your program. Donors are fans first, and they have chosen to spend their time with your program. They would be delighted to donate to help the program, if only you would let them do so by helping them understand what they could do. Building connections with donors takes time, so it is not feasible to do so with a large number of them. Five to ten committed donors should be enough to meet your program's needs.

You must be crystal clear with your donors, however, that they are giving their money with no strings attached. A parent giving money in hopes of ensuring their child gets playing time is an improper influence issue, not a donor issue.

HOW TO GET YOUR FIRST DONOR

Donors bring their friends and network with other donors. But what if you are new to a program and don't yet have your first donor?

To find your first donor, look at the fans who have already shown that they want to support the program. If you have a booster club like Utah's Block U club, it is virtually certain that your first donor is already a member. Club members have chosen to join so they can support the program and get extras above and beyond what a normal ticketholder would receive. Some of those who have already upgraded in this way may want to take the next step and become donors.

We suggest you end your first booster club dinner by letting the attendees know that you have a list of extras that would benefit the program but which aren't in the budget. Let the group know that if anyone is interested in helping out with the funding, they should send you an email. This is a gentle sell and is unlikely to offend anyone. But if there is someone in the club who would like to become a donor, you have opened the door for them.

DONORS TALK ABOUT DONORS

Anne and Lucy Osborn are sisters who are relatively new fans of Utah volleyball. Each has become a donor to the program, and they shared with us what drives them to give their money and their time.

Anne Osborn, MD (Distinguished Professor of Radiology at the University of Utah and Stanford women's basketball and swimming alumna) has traveled the world giving talks as the author of *Osborn's Brain*, one of the fundamental textbooks in radiology. Because of her travels, she was never able to be a season ticket holder or consistent fan of athletics. Lucy Osborn, MD (former Associate Vice President for Health Sciences at the University of Utah and retired professor of pediatrics) was also unable to be a fan while her career and family demanded her time.

The Osborn sisters became Utah volleyball fans three years ago when friends invited them to a match. They were immediately attracted to the "we rather than me" feel of the sport and were amazed at the athleticism and passion of the players. At this point, they were ready and willing to donate but were unsure how to get started.

Anne Osborn first became a donor when Beth was looking for help to pay for pedicures for her team before the NCAA Sweet Sixteen match at Stanford in 2019. Beth had heard her players talking about how badly they needed pedicures, but because they were so busy and didn't have the money, they hadn't had one in forever. She approached one of her regular donors to ask for funds, and that donor suggested she contact Anne as they thought she would relish the opportunity to contribute something the team would enjoy. Many donors become so because their friends bring them into the fold.

Anne's response to Beth's request was immediate and enthusiastic. She felt that paying for something fun for the players made her part of the family and increased her personal attachment to the team. Later on, Anne beamed when talking about the notes, hugs, texts, and photos she received from the players after the event. Heartfelt appreciation from the players is the best form of thanks you can give your donors.

Lucy Osborn became a donor by giving her time to make COVID-19 masks for the team. She obtained red Utah Utes branded fabrics and turned them into masks so the players could both look good and be safe. Other donors have given their time through leadership talks or by taking pictures for the team.

When asked about their generosity, the sisters gave interesting answers about why they gave and how they felt about it. In particular, Lucy was clear that donating was not about doing the program a favor. If that were the case, the program would be in their debt in some way. Instead, they felt they were donating to pay the team back for the joy and delight the program had given them. And, in their estimation, the program has given them quite a lot.

Now when they attend a match, they don't feel they are there just to be entertained at a sporting event. They feel like participants who have played a small part in the program's success. As professionals who have both had long and distinguished careers, they have found it rejuvenating to be included with the teenage and 20-something athletes. They see fan culture as an extension of team culture, and since the staff and players have been giving their all, they felt they should step up and do what they could do as well.

ADVICE FROM A MAJOR DONOR

Anne Osborn is also a major donor to other programs at the University of Utah and has raised funds for endowed faculty positions. Her advice as a donor above and beyond volleyball included:

- You can't be shy or embarrassed to ask for money. If you are, you won't get it.
- You need to be gracious and give people an out if they are not interested or able to contribute.
- It is rare that someone will give a large gift right out of the gate. Instead they give small gifts, see how it makes them feel, and then increase their giving as their connection increases. You need to think of donor development as a multiyear process, and you need to treasure your small donors as they may be tomorrow's large donors.
- Most people prefer to give for things they care about, so you need to listen to them and determine where their interests lie. What would get their juices flowing?
- What used to be called "Development" is better thought of as "Engagement."

Anne Osborn summed up her philosophy by telling a story of a friend asking if she could bring her dinner. Anne declined as she didn't want to be a bother. Her friend responded with a phrase that perfectly matches how Anne thinks about making donations:

"Would you deny me the pleasure of bringing you dinner?"

PLANNED GIFTS

At the top of the donor pyramid are planned gifts. These are agreements that donors include in their wills to ensure the program will receive a sizable donation upon their passing.

Harriet Hopf (Professor of Anesthesiology at the University of Utah, three-sport varsity athlete at Yale, and spouse of the co-author of this book) discussed the planned gift their family has made to women's athletics at the University of Utah. When their child reached adulthood, the Hopfs redid their wills and had to decide where to leave their funds. They first set aside money for their family, and then talked about what to do with the remainder.

Very quickly, they decided that they wanted to support women's athletics. Much of their social life revolved around attending women's volleyball, basketball, gymnastics, and softball matches, meets, and games, and they decided to contribute to the funding these programs richly deserve but don't always receive.

Thirty percent of their six-million-dollar gift will go to women's volleyball, thirty percent to women's basketball, and twenty percent to the Utes with Wings program, which donates to all of the university's women's intercollegiate sports. The remaining twenty percent will go to support women's club sports at the university.

This was not the first gift Harriet and her family had made to the program. They started with smaller donations to Utah volleyball for equipment and special events for the players. They went larger when they helped the Utes fund their summer European tour. This was a pivotal point in the relationship, and one that eventually contributed to them making their planned gift.

The volleyball coaches had invited the Hopfs to lunch to discuss fundraising for the European trip, and they enthusiastically agreed to contribute. But what really cemented the relationship was when the coaches said "we appreciate the funding, but the reason we asked you to lunch is to tell you that we want you to come with us!" The two weeks the Hopfs spent on the road with the team in Slovenia, Austria, the Czech Republic, and Italy was a milestone in their relationship with the staff and the players.

Beth and the other coaches did not have to wine and dine the Hopfs to obtain the planned gift. All they had to do was to welcome them into the program and make them feel like family.

MAIN POINTS IN THIS CHAPTER

- Your program can have a profound impact on the lives of your fans.
- Better facilities enhance the fan experience.
- It is a coach's responsibility to build a fan base and foster donor relationships.
- Booster clubs bridge the gaps between fans and donors.
- The donor-centric model enables those who love your program to support it financially and get pleasure from doing so.

CHAPTER 10: CRISIS MANAGEMENT AND COVID-19

"I wish it need not have happened in my time," said Frodo.

"So do I," said Gandalf, "and so do all who live to see such times. But that is not for them to decide. All we have to decide is what to do with the time that is given us."

From "The Fellowship of the Ring" by J.R.R. Tolkien

Everyone has struggled with crisis management during the COVID-19 pandemic and wished it had not happened in our time. When the virus hit, the situation evolved rapidly, and it was hard to know what was coming next, much less how to prepare for it. When the shutdown orders came, coaches had less than a week to shift to a remote program from the in-person program they had been running all their lives.

Teams at all levels were affected. The NBA placed its season on hold and other professional sports quickly followed. Colleges and universities went virtual over a weekend, volleyball clubs were shut down, and schools closed and went online. Besides having to figure out how to lead and manage a program virtually, the financial toll was tremendous. At every level, costs continued even as revenues dried up.

The pain intensified, with little help in sight. No one who is a coach today has ever lived through a pandemic, so there were no best practices, lessons learned, or storehouses of knowledge to provide guidance on how to lead and manage your way out of the situation that had been thrust upon you. People scrambled and did their best, but there were so many things that needed to be done; it was overwhelming. And it was easy to lose sight of the progress you were making because there was always more to do. As Tara VanDerveer, Stanford women's basketball coach, told us:

> "COVID-19 puts things in perspective. Highly accomplished people celebrate finding a pack of toilet paper."

While coaching during a pandemic was an entirely new experience, some lessons can be taken from leading during other crises. Jay Lund, CEO of Andersen Corporation, highlighted the unique aspects of the pandemic while incorporating tried and true lessons in his approach when he told us:

> "If I have learned one thing from this crisis, it is when there is so much uncertainty and so little we control, we as leaders must be clear, decisive, agile and humble—we are going to make mistakes, but we must keep moving forward and get smarter and better each day. And of course, we must communicate often and with honesty, confidence, and hope."

FORMAL VS. INFORMAL INTERACTIONS

The COVID-19 crisis forced virtually all communication to go from informal to formal. In normal times, Beth stays connected with her staff through Management by Walking Around (MBWA). She likes to hold frequent informal meetings and holds few structured ones. But the COVID-19 crisis greatly reduced the opportunity for informal connection. Now, everything had to be structured and scheduled.

Beth's usual approach was to go into the office in the morning and stop by the desk of each staff member to ask how things were going and what she could do to help. This informal communication enabled anyone to raise an issue without needing to prepare for a formal meeting. This ensured issues were raised as soon as they came up rather than letting them grow as they would have if Beth had not made herself available.

But with nobody in the office, there was no one to drop in on. Instead, everything now needed to be scheduled. Whether it was Zoom, Skype, Google Hangouts, or Facebook Video Chat, everything had a scheduled start and end time. Soon it became routine—click a link, chat, click the link for the next meeting.

Hour after hour of scheduled meetings piled up one on top of another. Though this is the norm in the business world, for those in athletics clicking one link after the other and staring into a computer screen all day was a huge shift. "My Eyes Glaze Over" (MEGO) became standard operating procedure, and people began longing for the days when you could just drop by the office next door and informally chat rather than having to schedule a meeting for even the smallest of topics.

Dan Corotan, University of Utah volleyball assistant coach, noted the absence of informal conversations when he said:

"The informal drop-ins created organic conversations you didn't know you were going to have. They led to useful tangents and made it easy to bounce ideas off of each other."

Online video technology services worked surprisingly well given the enormous increase in usage they experienced when in-person contact was shut down. For example, Zoom experienced a 728% increase in first-time installations in the five weeks starting March 2, 2020. But, although traffic exploded, the platform remained stable.

CRISES ARE OVER-MANAGED AND UNDER-LED

It is tempting to try to manage a crisis and impose order on it. But by their very nature, crises are not business as usual, and simply applying normal organizing principles won't work. Instead, leadership is needed to provide direction and hope, even when the leader isn't sure exactly how things will play out. In a crisis, you may not always know the best path, but you must always project calm and confidence that things will work out.

Crisis management requires the following skills from leaders, not all of which may come naturally to you:

- Unleash your creativity. Since there are no standard operating procedures to handle a crisis, you will need to free up everyone's creativity to meet new and unexpected challenges.

- Be humble and transparent. Nobody knows how the crisis will eventually be solved. Spend more time listening, testing, and learning and less time trying to prove you were right.
- Address multiple stakeholders. Your athletic director, staff, players, and their parents will all have different issues and concerns. You need to talk to each group about the things they find most important.
- Communicate excessively and honestly. If there is bad news to share, don't sugar coat it or hide it. Treat your team as adults and let them know the truth. The need for communication goes up during a crisis, and it will be highly unlikely that you will err by communicating too much. On the other hand, confusion can result if each coach sends multiple emails and texts every day, so it is critical to coordinate communication, identify leaders for specific areas, and reduce unnecessary messages.
- Accept uncertainty. The rate of change in a crisis is much faster than the rate of change in normal times. The world is more uncertain, and fighting the uncertainty won't make it go away.
- Be agile and flexible. People typically think of agility as making changes to your system, while flexibility means working within your current system. Because the world changes so quickly during a crisis, you must be prepared to accelerate your decision-making and actions. This is especially difficult since you are dealing with more uncertainty than you normally face.
- Celebrate small wins. It is easy for people's spirits to get down during a crisis. Look for small wins that can remind people that there is always something to appreciate.
- Identify opportunities. It is tempting to see only the downside of a crisis since that is what is directly in your

face. But crises provide lessons (such as maintaining your program while reducing travel) that can pay off once the crisis has passed.

THERE HAVE BEEN CRISES BEFORE COVID-19

As everyone is struggling to deal with the COVID-19 crisis, it is helpful to remember that crises have struck programs before the epidemic. The difference with COVID-19 is that it came on almost overnight and happened for all programs at the same time.

In 2007, the Utah program faced a crisis of its own. Utah was returning all of its players after going 16-0 in the Mountain West Conference (MWC) the previous year, and there was a consensus amongst coaches that the Utes were set to make a run to the Final Four. But it was not to be. The two best players went to a developmental tryout in February, and when they came back, they announced they wanted to transfer. Someone from somewhere had told them they needed to play in a bigger conference. This was before the transfer portal existed and when transferring was not common.

There were plenty of theories in the volleyball world at the time as to exactly what had led to this. Since Utah had experienced almost no transfers before or since, this was a big topic of concern for many coaches.

More importantly, it was a crushing blow to Utah's returning players. They were devastated and felt betrayed. Beth's concern about the transfers quickly turned to concern about the players that remained. She circled the wagons to protect the returning players from the rumors that were flying around and to provide them with space to mourn. It felt tragic at the time and was a big hit to the program.

That summer, Utah's other top player tore her ACL and was out for the year. The Utes entered the 2007 season without its three top players with a schedule that was the second toughest in the country. The Utes had put together a strong schedule to prepare the team for a deep NCAA tournament run.

It was not an easy year, but Beth has never been prouder of a team for persevering and coming out of the season better than they started. Utah ended up three points from getting into the NCAA tournament, having lost 15-12 in the 5th set of the MWC Championship, costing them the automatic bid. Utah also needed that win to get over 500 in order to qualify for the tournament. Had the Utes been even one match over 500, they would have gotten an at-large bid due to the strength of their schedule.

Among other actions to help the team deal with the transfers and the injury, Beth did the following:

- Held listening sessions at team meetings in the locker room to let the players vent their anger, frustration, and hurt.
- Put together an entirely new lineup. Beth moved their libero to setter until the backup setter had gained more experience in practice.
- Avoided engaging in the media about the issues surrounding the transfers. This was particularly challenging in 2008 when Utah went to the Sweet Sixteen and the two players who had transferred also made it to that level on their new teams and were at the same site as Utah. The media pushed hard for negative comments, but Beth and the team kept their opinions to themselves.

So, while the COVID-19 crisis is new, teams have faced and dealt with crises in the past.

COMMUNICATING PROGRESS DURING A CRISIS

Four weeks into the crisis, Beth composed a long note to her Athletics Director, Mark Harlan, and her Associate Athletic Director, Nona Richardson, to update them on the progress the volleyball program had made in learning how to lead and manage their program remotely. The initial purpose of this note was to inform her bosses, but by compiling all their activities into one place, it also gave the volleyball staff confidence that they had been making significant progress.

One additional benefit from Beth updating her bosses was that her example was picked up by a member of the staff who began doing a much better job of updating Beth than they had done previously.

Some of the subjects to address were one-time-only urgent matters, such as getting the players home to their families when the school shut down. Others, such as developing routine and structure remotely, were ongoing and could be applied to any remote situation, both now and in the future. There were so many subjects to cover, however, it was hard to know what to do first. A tool from psychology—Maslow's Hierarchy of Needs—provided an organizing structure for what should be done immediately and what should follow.

TOOL: MASLOW'S HIERARCHY OF NEEDS

One of the key concepts in psychology is Maslow's Hierarchy of Needs. When you first read about it in Psych 101, it probably sounded pretty theoretical. But in a crisis, it becomes a surprisingly useful guide as to what needs to be done and in what order.

Here is the pyramid showing the hierarchy of needs:

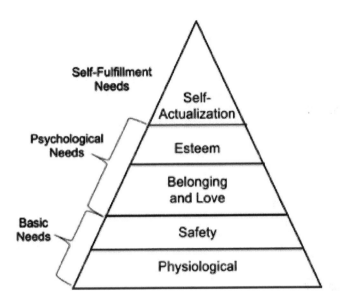

Figure 10-1: Maslow's Hierarchy of Needs

It is a waste of time to try to satisfy needs at the top of the pyramid if the needs at the bottom of the hierarchy are unmet. You must first satisfy the basic needs, then satisfy the psychological needs, and finally, if there is time and money left over, go after self-actualization.

Beth's email to her bosses can be mapped onto Maslow's hierarchy. She addressed the issues by beginning at the bottom and then moving up as she led her staff and players though the early stages of the COVID-19 crisis.

Figure 10-2: Beth's application of Maslow's hierarchy

MEETING BASIC PHYSIOLOGICAL AND SAFETY NEEDS

Figure 10-3: Basic needs

Food, shelter, and safety were the first and most urgent issues to be addressed when the university shut down the school and the dorms. The first week after the shutdown was focused on the physical and mental health of the players. The staff made sure every player had secure housing and access to food. After one week, all of the players had made it home to their families, including getting one of the players back to their home in Hungary.

MEETING PSYCHOLOGICAL BELONGINGNESS AND LOVE NEEDS

Figure 10-4: Psychological needs

The next level of needs requires reminding everyone that they are connected, they belong, and that you care about them. The isolation required during a pandemic pushes in the opposite direction and tends to make people feel they are on their own with no one to help them out.

Academics. Once the athletes were safe, the program took actions to ensure the players stayed on top of their academics. Like colleges and universities, athletes had to adapt to going virtual in the span of a long weekend. It would have been easy, and perhaps natural, to feel that everything in their life had gone out of control which would lead to them feeling helpless and untethered.

By focusing on their academics early on, the players had one thing that gave continuity to their lives. Their classes switched to online, but because they were in the middle of the semester, they were continuing their classes rather than being uprooted and having to start something new. The staff chose to add very little else onto the athletes' plates so they had one clear target on which to focus. With so much changing, it was nice to have at least one thing that just moved ahead pretty much as it had been.

In addition, connecting the players with their academic advisors, mentors, and tutors enabled them to continue the relationships that had supported them before the crisis. Utah's academic advisor, Mary Chris Finnegan, was a stable force for the players during this time. This continuity also helped the players deal with their emotions during the abrupt transition.

One-on-one calls. Beth did a round of 30-minute one-on-one phone calls to spend time with each assistant, staff member, and player. Beth's primary job during these phone calls was just to listen. These calls hardly mentioned volleyball. Instead, the calls were about family, academics, friends, and safety. The calls addressed their concerns and fears, and Beth reminded them of the psychology and wellness resources that mental health professionals Jonathan Ravarino and Uma Dorn provided to assist them through this unsettling period.

Beth used the Kübler-Ross model (denial, anger, depression, bargaining, acceptance) to help everyone understand the phases of dealing with the changes being forced upon them. Different people were in different stages, and having a framework made it more acceptable to openly discuss the stage each person found themselves in.

The first round of one-on-one calls was to help settle everyone into their changed reality. More rounds of calls would be needed as people moved to different stages of the Kübler-Ross model. It also became clear that some people needed much more time to feel connected than others, so flexibility in scheduling was critical.

Communication. Eventually, the time came to start communicating with the entire group. The program used Team Works and Zoom to hold meetings with the staff and players. These were necessary so that everyone heard the same thing and stayed on the same page.

To enhance the sense of routine, the meetings followed a schedule. Initially, the staff met daily and the team met weekly, bringing in additional support staff as needed.

It didn't take long before the energy started to fade due to the frequency of meetings. Spacing the meetings out a bit meant people looked forward to them and had the energy and bandwidth to be present and focused on the discussion at hand. One of the advantages of using video chat is that you can easily pick up when people fade out and begin looking at their phones. Adjusting in real time to meeting fatigue was a valuable lesson of the pandemic.

Connection. Once the initial crisis had been dealt with, it was time to shift gears to reconnect the group and return to some semblance of a team. Players and staff were communicating daily through the Team Works app. Staff members were also given Box folders (Box is a file sharing program similar to Dropbox) to upload videos about nutrition, workouts, volleyball, fun, etc. for the players to access.

Social media. It was important to let recruits, fans, and friends know the Utah volleyball program was still functioning during this difficult period. The staff shared great memories from the past year by posting pictures and videos on Twitter, Facebook, and Instagram. They created an "a day in the life" series highlighting student-athletes and shared stories about how the support staff were getting along. They also shared the inspiring stories of Utah alumnae who were currently working in medical fields and active on the front lines responding to the COVID-19 pandemic.

Routine and structure. The players needed to be educated quickly on the importance of routine and structure for their physical and mental health. It would have been easy for them to drift aimlessly without the discipline a routine enforced. Utah's Director of Sports Science, Ernie Rimer, got on a team Zoom and did a fun video routine with his family that served as an example of what a healthy routine looked like.

Figure 10-5: COVID-19 routine

Tom Farden, Utah gymnastics coach, noted:

"Clear communication is the cornerstone to achieving success. I also feel that consistency is somewhat of a lost art. That is why even during this pandemic, we held our staff meeting on Mondays and our recruiting meetings on Tuesdays."

Budgeting. Like virtually every other program, the University of Utah took a financial hit when it closed down in-person activities. This led to across-the-board budget cuts for all sports that needed to be made quickly. Since the bulk of the costs of the program are its people, Beth needed to work the numbers hard to make sure she took care of her staff and the student-athletes. She had to make painful cuts in many areas of her operation but did not make them in areas that would affect members of her program. These cuts enabled her to keep everyone in the program employed and, hopefully, continue to give the players a great student-athlete experience as part of a nationally competitive program.

MEETING PSYCHOLOGICAL ESTEEM NEEDS

Once everyone's need to feel they were valued and cared for had been taken care of, the focus shifted back to their athletics.

Volleyball Performance Team. This group was critical early on for strategizing the next moves once things settled down. The volleyball performance team meets, without fail, every week. The membership includes the volleyball coaching staff, Henry Ruggiero and Emma Ostermann (sports performance), Ernie Rimer (sports science), Lindsey Adams (athletic trainer), Maria Di Iorio (sports nutritionist), and Uma Dorn (mental health and performance).

The Utah Volleyball Performance Team is arguably one of the most knowledgeable, active, and efficient groups in the country. This team helps guide the program with science, planning, and communication. They use systematic planning, known as periodization, that incorporates every aspect of the athletes' training (volleyball training, strength and conditioning, practice and match jump counts, practice planning, injuries, mental health, etc.)

The coaches work collaboratively with this group and value their expertise and input. They are a finely tuned team that functions at a very high level, truly cares about the program and its players, and works hard to keep the program at the national forefront of research and execution.

At times during COVID-19, this team spent more time with the players than did the coaching staff. In particular, they were in constant communication with players concerning their home workouts. This group was also instrumental in developing the return-to-play plan and defining how to apply sports science to keep the players healthy and injury free when the team returned to the gym.

Physical training. After about three weeks, the staff thought the players could emotionally handle working out. The strength coach sent workout plans to the players, and she created her own communication system with them. The staff also sent care packages to each player with strength bands, a volleyball, and a motivational laminated visual of the team's goals and vision.

Figure 10-6: Workout care packages

Figure 10-7: Motivational visual aid in the care packages

The University of Utah has an impressive performance center on campus with a complete array of equipment and space tailored to the needs of its athletes, but the athletes were home with their families, not at the University. The players sent pictures of their home workout equipment, which ranged from rather impressive modern workout rooms to rusty backyard barbells lying in the dirt for pumping iron old-school. The program worked with each player individually to tailor workouts that were possible given the equipment they had at hand.

DISC behavioral styles. The University of Utah volleyball program employs the DISC behavioral style tool to identify individual behavioral styles for all staff and athletes (covered in Chapter 6). To help the staff understand how to help each individual player during the COVID crisis based on their behavioral style, a DISC professional was invited on staff zooms. This same person was invited to join numerous Zoom meetings with the team to help them understand the emotions they were experiencing. The staff also held separate small group meetings with the 2019 first years who had not had time to be educated on DISC during the busy academic year but who now could spend time to understand this important tool.

MEETING SELF-ACTUALIZATION NEEDS

Figure 10-8: Self-Actualization needs

After everyone's self-esteem needs were met to the extent possible during the crisis, the next step was to move on to the topics that would help realize everyone's full potential.

Reassuring current players. The coaches called all of the current players to make sure they had everything they needed to come back when the university allowed it. The magnitude of the disruption on the lives of the young adults had been enormous, and the program was prepared to do all they could to support its players.

Inspiration. Beth felt the weight of the situation taking its toll on everyone. She wanted to introduce something out of the ordinary to serve as a reminder that there was more to life than just hard slogging and making it through each day.

During one virtual meeting, the team was surprised with a Zoom visit by Justin Su'a, a performance psychologist and motivational speaker who the team loves. They listen to his podcasts in normal times, and they were delighted to have a chance to speak with him in (virtual) person. The team's energy when they saw him on Zoom was palpable. It gave everyone a shot of positivity just when they needed it the most.

Su'a talked to the team about people being either fountains who fill your life up or drains who bring you down. You want more fountains in your life, and it is up to you to choose who to let in. Here are more of Su'a 's ideas from his Twitter account:

> "Examine the patterns of your day-to-day life and see what you should stop doing, start doing, and keep doing."

> "When you change the way you look at things, the things you look at change."

Recruiting. Recruiting was put on the back burner during the initial crisis when the program was dealing with other needs on Maslow's hierarchy. Recruiting is obviously fundamental to any program's success, but there just wasn't any capacity to give it much time.

The coaches began the recruiting push by calling the club directors with whom they had the strongest ties. The initial conversations weren't about individual players. Instead, the calls focused on how the club directors and their families were doing. Though Utah's program had made it towards the top of the hierarchy of needs, it was clear that many of the clubs were still dealing with basic needs and survival. Club directors are running a business, and the reduction of revenue caused by COVID-19 has been devastating to their livelihoods.

Eventually, Utah staff shifted more of their energy toward communicating with recruits by phone calls and Zoom. Since in-person recruiting was put on hold indefinitely, the challenge was to figure out how to help recruits learn as much as possible about the Utah program virtually rather than in-person. It was challenging at first, but like everything else during the COVID-19 crisis, everyone adjusted and found a way to make it work.

OTHER ITEMS FOR THE UNIVERSITY OF UTAH

Though everything felt so different when COVID-19 hit, the world still went on and time still marched by. There were many important and ongoing topics that remained to be dealt with once there was some breathing room.

Many of these have been made more challenging with the uncertainty of what would be opening when. For example, the staff had to move full speed ahead and plan for summer camps before knowing whether or not they would be held. And if the camps ended up being virtual, the staff needed to develop a plan on exactly how that would work. Eventually, the 2020 summer camps were cancelled, but the planning had to happen before that call was made.

Though exactly what would be allowed when the season arrived was unclear, there were several planning items that could not wait. The staff needed to prepare and sign the contracts necessary for making everything happen should the season begin in the fall. When the season was postponed, all of the match contracts became null and void based on a clause relating to "uncontrollable forces."

The Utah volleyball program has a leadership group consisting of four current players that met online regularly. They have formed small groups of teammates to communicate better, offered support and messaging, and taken the lead in setting the season goals for the program. The staff knew this was a key time for leadership development and took the opportunity to mentor, guide, and encourage this group to actively engage with and provide leadership to their teammates during the crisis.

This group continued to be a great resource for the staff during these difficult times. Valuable feedback from them included issues such as, "what is the mental state of the team?" and "would the team be in favor of moving forward with a fall or spring season if it meant reduced matches and a watered-down championship without fans?"

As it turned out, they did not have to answer the second question because the NCAA decided competitions would not count against any player for the 2020-2021 season. If teams want to try to play and get stopped by COVID-19 concerns, at least it won't cost players a year of eligibility.

The staff reached out to the fans and donor base. They sent links to a highlight and thank you video to the Block U fan club members and held a Zoom chat between coaches, select players, and season ticket holders. No one knows how many fans will be allowed to attend matches or what the rules for them will be, but the coaches wanted to make sure every fan knows they are valued.

In order to stay in touch with the fans, Utah's communications team stepped up their social media game. Because there were no matches on which to report, the communications team had to get creative and reported on great moments from the past and gave more details about the players and coaches.

Finally, the coaches made special efforts to contact donors and potential donors. Though the team always appreciates their generosity, in this year donors may be particularly critical. The revised budget (as all sports at the University of Utah were required to do) cut out all of the niceties in order to have enough money to retain everyone on staff and to keep operating at a nationally competitive level. The resulting budget has none of the special events that serve to brighten players' spirits and break the tension of the season. If any of these are to be added back in, it will have to be done courtesy of donations made by those who love and support the program.

OTHER ITEMS FOR COACHES

Beth is a big believer in giving back to the sport. And in some ways, being under isolation has helped her give back to volleyball even more than normal. Beth and Leo had talked about writing this book for several years but had never found the time. Because neither of us could travel during this crisis, we finally were able to make the time to write it.

We have also been doing online presentations on the topics in this book for coaches' groups such as the AVCA and WeCoach. The questions arising from the coaches during these presentations informed many of the ideas we have addressed in this book.

RAMPING UP TRAINING

Even in the midst of the uncertainty caused by the virus, the players returned to campus and continued to train. To do so safely, the University of Utah created numerous protocols and a phased approach. In each phase, players were allowed to do more activities in conjunction with others.

The first phase only allowed one person lifting with the strength coach 10 feet away and single person drills on the volleyball court. Eventually they were able to transition into small group activities and finally able to play live six vs. six. Players are permitted to access their locker room to use the restrooms and change before and after practice but are not allowed to linger as they normally would.

Utah has a modern training center that all of the athletics teams use (except for football, which has its own dedicated facility). The equipment and machines from the training center have been decentralized across the athletic facilities. For example, one of the three volleyball courts in Utah's practice facility has been transformed into a temporary weight room.

No one wanted to have times like this with the challenges they bring. But since the times have been given to us, the best everyone can do is to safely take things one step at a time and move towards whatever the new normal turns out to be.

HOW COVID-19 IS CHANGING ATHLETICS

After the first month of COVID-19, things seemed to settle in a bit. The pandemic had shut down just about everything by mid-March, and by the end of April people had fallen into their new routines of staying at home and working on video calls, and had settled in for the long haul. It seemed we would be running a marathon in which everyone would get into a consistent rhythm, but that is not what happened.

Instead, there were ebbs and flows as the days and weeks lingered on. NCAA legislation, which normally takes years to change, was changing daily. On one day, coaches and athletes believed there would be a fall season, and the next, that belief was challenged with news report of the virus numbers escalating. There was widespread exhaustion and frustration, bordering on depression. Player meetings went from positive to negative as the reality of what was happening began to sink in and motivation began to wane.

In the end, when the Pac-12 cancelled all fall 2020 sports, Beth gave her players, coaches, and support staff 10 days off to regroup and mourn the loss of a season.

The many protocols the University and Athletic Department put in place for the athletes to return to campus seem to have worked. Investing in a robust testing program was expensive but necessary. The need for social distancing, hand washing, and mask wearing are discussed with athletes daily. Players wearing masks while they train is mandatory, and it is officially the new era of sport.

The staff scheduled one day a week in the office to work on the things best handled in-person. They wear masks and practice social distancing from their co-workers when on office visits. They will continue to work remotely on the other days while keeping in mind the need to stay connected while out of the office.

During the quarantine, sports channels broadcast reruns of classic moments in sport. Watching sport coverage from even a year ago is unsettling. Now, seeing athletes high-five, chest bump, and hug brings up an involuntary reaction of "What were they thinking? Where is the distancing?" Watching fans interact with players appears unsafe from the new perspective.

There is anxiety about returning to in-person jobs after isolating at home for months. Sport requires long hours with immense intensity, and coaches and athletes were not used to being home for so much time. Existing in a highly competitive world with travel as the norm is a way of life, but after many months at home, it seems a bit daunting. Even the most seasoned professionals were wondering if they had lost a step or gotten a bit rusty after being isolated for so long.

We have learned a lot about COVID-19 and public health. But there is much less definition around how to play sports safely. Here is a sampling of the outstanding questions about athletic competition:

• How long will athletes have to wear masks to practice?

- Will organizations attempt to create "bubbles" as the NBA and WNBA have successfully done?
- Will athletes be required to wear masks during games and matches? How will that affect their performance? Will they be allowed to huddle closely, or will they be forced to spread out?
- What will happen when one or more athletes or staff members test positive for COVID-19?
- Will fans be allowed at the competitions? If so, how many fans will be allowed? How close to the court will they be allowed to sit? Will they be required to wear masks? What is the social-distancing plan for fans? What will the workers do if fans refuse to abide by these rules?
- Will other groups, such as bands, cheerleaders, and dance groups be allowed to perform at games and matches?
- Will coaches have to wear masks? Will they be able to remove them for interviews with television commentators? For that matter, will commentators be located at the venue or will they be calling the games from a studio or even from home?
- What will airline travel for the staff and team look like? Will the program pay extra to fly on airlines that take safety more seriously?
- Will programs pay for coaches and staff who are older than 60 to fly first class to provide them with additional protection since their age puts them at higher risk for COVID-19?
- How many wipes and disinfectants will the team need to secure to supply the travel party?
- How will the team secure food on the road that is both safe and nutritious?
- What protocols will teams enact when they get to a

hotel? Will players have their own rooms? If budgetary restrictions preclude single rooms, how will you decide on who to you put together as roommates?

Staff and athletes are good at seeing problems and solving them through creativity and hard work. This makes a situation such as COVID-19 particularly difficult for these highly competitive people. No matter how hard they try, they cannot just find a way to win. COVID-19 is a problem without many short-term solutions and that brings plenty of pain to go around.

Beth tells her athletes, "keep your head up and your nose down," meaning stay positive, but do the work necessary to keep yourself and those around you healthy and safe and ready to play. It will take time for the uncertainties to resolve, and patience will be necessary.

COVID-19'S IMPACT NOW THAT THE 2020 SEASON HAS BEEN DELAYED

No one knows how the COVID-19 crisis will play out. But you must continue moving forward the best you can in the face of that uncertainty. All Pac-12 sports have been delayed until at least January, 2021. When teams will be allowed to play again is currently unknown. What is known is that there are many issues that will arise because of delaying the season. These include:

- When might the fall sport season actually occur, and how can you keep your team close to readiness should it be scheduled with minimal advanced notice?
- If the season occurs in the spring, how will you handle conflicts with other sports playing in their normal seasons?

- How will the players react to having to sit out a year? Will your seniors graduate and leave, or will they stay around for their last season?
- When athletes, parents, and prospects ask you what will happen, what will you tell them, given you don't really know yourself?
- How much of your budget will be reduced and when will you get back what has been cut?
- Scholarships will be untouched but compensation for staff is at risk. Will staff members such as the director of operations, managers, and technical directors be retained? Will there be furloughs? If so, for whom and how long will they last? What about the consultants your program has relied on in the past?
- What will your scholarship distribution look like in the future? Season cancellations will allow players to redshirt, but how will you deal with fifth-year aid in the future for so many players?
- What will the season look like when it finally begins? The schedule may be changed to reduce travel, particularly air travel. Fans may or may not be allowed in the arenas. Uncertainty abounds.
- How will the uncertainty in start time of the season affect your incoming first years? How will it affect the decisions of the recruits in your pipeline?
- How will you stay in contact with fans now that there won't be a fall season? How will you keep them as enthusiastic supporters of your program?

How organized a program is during this uncertain time will be critical to its future success. Being designed to win, even in a pandemic, will pay off when play resumes. Programs that keep up communication, have clearly defined roles, and have systems in place to mitigate the uncertainty will come out of the pandemic better positioned to win.

WHAT COVID-19 LESSONS CAN WE CARRY FORWARD?

Eventually, the COVID-19 crisis will lessen and the world will transition to a new normal. But since no one knows exactly when that will be or what that will look like, programs need to be pre-pared for a wide variety of possible outcomes. Those could in-clude a return of the virus, a vaccine that effectively eliminates the virus, or anything in between.

The need for preparedness and making the shift from in-person to virtual may arise again. If so, now there is a template to follow. But even in the new normal, there are ways we can take advantage of what we have learned. Some possibilities might include:

- How could you reduce recruiting trips that require two to three days of travel and instead watch more online video to evaluate players? Will high schools and clubs continue to set up cameras to stream online practices and competitions?
- Without a doubt, there will be times when you will want to fly out to show key recruits you are interested in them, but can recruiting travel be reduced for safety and cost?
- How could you incorporate Maslow's Hierarchy of Needs into your thinking so you are not trying to satisfy higher-level needs before lower-level needs have been fulfilled?
- How could you leverage your budget to engage a specialist or consultant for a one-hour video call rather than having to bring them in and paying for a full day of their time?

- How could you apply some of the same technologies and approaches you have been using with your staff and players to connect more closely with your fan base? After all, a head coach could reach hundreds of fans at once and have it feel like a semi-private chat using Zoom or another video meeting technology.
- How could you make constant communication up and down in the organization a norm even when everyone is back in the same location?
- How could you hold the gain on social media so that it still holds interest above and beyond simply reporting final scores?

Everyone will be delighted once the COVID-19 crisis is brought under control. Even so, there are lessons people can take from the painful necessity of dealing with the crisis which will help in the coming years.

MAIN POINTS IN THIS CHAPTER

- The balance between formal vs. informal interactions was upset by the COVID-19 crisis.
- Crises are over-managed and under-led.
- There have been many crises before COVID-19, but they hit individual programs, not all teams at the same time.
- Maslow's hierarchy of needs provides guidance as to what should come first and what should follow during a crisis.
- COVID-19 is changing athletics, and it is not yet clear what the end game will look like.
- There are lessons learned from the COVID-19 crisis that will benefit programs when the world returns to a new normal.

CHAPTER 11: PREPARING FOR THE FUTURE

"When the world is going to change—be the first one out of the gate and figure it out."

John Dunning (five-time NCAA volleyball champion and American Volleyball Coaches Association Hall of Famer)

The world is changing faster than it was, and it will be changing faster still tomorrow. Advances in technology and improvements in the analysis of big data enable insights that simply weren't available in the past. These changes are disrupting all activities, whether they be in athletics, business, medicine, or the arts.

The important question to ask yourself is how fast you and your program are changing relative to the world around you. If the world moves faster than you do, you will find parts of your program are better prepared for the world as it was, rather than for how it will be. To be designed to win you must be designed for the world of today and tomorrow, not the world of yesterday.

How do you prepare for the future when no one knows what the future will hold? Trying to predict exactly what will happen guarantees that you will fail. The goal, however, is not to try and predict exactly what will happen. Instead, you should be looking for broad trends that tell you in which direction things are changing. The tool that helps identify these trends is called the radar screen.

TOOL: THE RADAR SCREEN

Everyone has seen movies with submarines using radar. The operator watches the screen to seek out early warnings of potential threats around the sub. The blips on the screen might be an enemy sub, a school of fish, a massive boulder, or an underwater cliff. In any case, wise submariners react to the blip so they can be ready before the threat is on top of them.

Your program has a radar screen that shows the things you could spend time addressing. Most of your time is spent on the dead center of your screen asking the question "What urgent items do I have to react to now?" Perhaps a player sprains an ankle the night before a big match and you need to switch up your lineup. On an even shorter scale, you may call a time-out to deal with two shanked passes in a row early in the fifth set. You could easily fill up your entire day dealing with nothing but the urgent blips.

Figure 11-1: The radar screen

While those urgent issues are important, it is a great invest-ment of your time to ask two forward-looking questions using the radar screen. The first is "What is on the outside moving in?" These blips are trends that are not yet greatly affecting today's day-to-day activities but might affect them mightily in the coming months or years. They are the things you will need to deal with for next season and the season after that.

The second question is "What is on the inside moving out?" These blips are things that used to be true or relevant but are becoming less so over time and are starting to feel a bit stale and old-fashioned. If you do not make changes, your coaching and your program will begin to feel dated and out of touch, and you will be stuck in the past.

If the actions you take are consistent with the blips you see on the radar screen, you are headed where the world is going. You are a boat on a rising tide. If you are going in a different direction than the radar screen, with each passing season you will get far-ther and farther away from where you need to be.

An important point to remember is that the radar screen is not about you. It is about the world around you. Later in this chapter, we will address the separate question of how fast you are changing relative to the world around you.

RADAR SCREEN EXAMPLES

Here are some examples of the radar screen in different settings so you can get a feel for the tool before we apply it to athletics.

In the auto industry:

- Outside moving in: Tesla's high-performance luxury vehicles that fully utilize the advantages that electric motors possess over internal combustion engines.
- Inside moving out: Tame, low-performing electric cars with small batteries and short ranges between charges.

When electric vehicles first came out, people bought them to make a statement about protecting the planet by reducing emissions. They were sold as a way of feeling good about your environmental sensitivity by driving a minimally acceptable car. Driving an electric car meant trade-offs in range, power, and comfort.

That approach no longer works. Tesla changed the game by entering the market with roomy cars that had far better performance than brands such as Porsche or Ferrari. Just as a comparison, here are a few numbers:

- 0–60 mph time: Tesla S P100D, 2.28 seconds. Ferrari LaFerrari, 2.4 seconds.
- Seating: Tesla S seats seven comfortably, LaFerrari seats two.
- Price: The Tesla is less than 1/10th the cost of the LaFerrari.

If you are still trying to sell an underpowered, short-range electric car, you are stuck in the past.

In the grocery industry:

- Outside moving in: Extreme transparency in how protein was raised, fed, and cared for; locally sourced, organic/natural products; streamlined payment technology; curbside touchless pickup.
- Inside moving out: Food additives in a "clean label" world (clean label means as close to natural as possible), personal interactions at checkout.

The implications of these trends are that if you are selling meat with unclear sourcing and trying to delight your customers with chatty checkout personnel, you are living in the past. Each year will get more and more difficult for you because the world is moving in one direction and you are moving in another.

It is the same in athletics. The world is changing around you, and if you do not change as fast or faster, you will become stuck in the past and your program will be at risk of becoming irrelevant. Your recruiting will suffer because athletes will feel that other programs are more attuned to their needs, while your program will feel more like one in which their parents might have competed.

NCAA SPORTS RADAR SCREEN:
OUTSIDE MOVING IN

Figure 11-2: Radar screen: outside moving in

Blips on the outside moving in are not yet affecting your program but may start doing so quite quickly. Here is a starter set of the current blips for NCAA programs (Most of these examples will be relevant to all sports):

- Name, Image, and Likeness (NIL): This new NCAA rule will allow student-athletes to earn money based on their fame as athletes. Its consequences are extremely hard to predict.

- Analytics in sport: The Moneyball approach of analyzing large sets of data to determine what is and is not effective will play an increasingly larger role in recruiting, training, and scouting. The accumulated data can be graphed, charted, and analyzed to create insights of all kinds.

- Applying sports science with performance teams: This will optimize the training of your student-athletes. We described Utah's Volleyball Performance Team in Chapter 10.

- Neuroscience and learning how to learn and teach: Neuroscience is the field that studies the mechanisms of how the brain learns and develops. By using these insights, training can be enhanced to match the brain's and body's optimal pathways for improvement.

- Understanding and educating the entire program on diversity and racial equality so that every team member feels welcome and included: Your players are attuned to all types of social issues, and it is the coach's responsibility as part of the educational process to make sure there are conversations and actions on even the most difficult of these topics.

- Players bringing outside leadership concepts: It used to be that leadership was taught top-down from coach to player. Now, players are bringing in ideas from their high school classes and teams, leadership programs, books, podcasts, and numerous online sources. There are so many channels for information that limiting it to the coaches unnecessarily restricts the flow. What matters are the quality of the ideas, not who brings them into the program.

- Mental health and performance: College athletics bring pressure and visibility that can be hard for players to handle. More student-athletes are arriving with more diagnosed mental health issues than has been the case in the past. A strong mental health program shows that the athletic department truly cares about the athletes. In addition, better mental health leads to better performance.

- Entering college with overuse injuries: Student-athletes are entering college with overuse injuries from year-round training in their primary sport, intense seasons, and minimal cross-training in different sports. This excess focus may help them win a scholarship, but it leads to unbalanced muscle groups and aggravates ligaments, muscles, and joints at younger and younger ages.

- Individualization of training: As sports science increases in capability, training can be focused more specifically on the student-athlete's individual mentality, physique, and nutritional needs. Training will no longer be one-size-fits-all.

- Increased use of the transfer portal (both in and out): Before the transfer portal, student-athletes would need to create their own process for transferring schools and might need to sit out for a year after they transferred. The portal has simplified the process and will lead to more and more transfers. You can't rest on your laurels once you have recruited a student-athlete; re-recruitment will be a staple of keeping them in your program.

- Money, resources, and expectations are going up: Though budgets will always be tight, more money will enter programs as visibility and expectations rise. College athletics are in competition with professional sports, concerts, movies, and other entertainment activities, and must earn the attention of paying customers.

- Changes to recruiting rules: The NCAA has changed recruiting rules so that elite young athletes cannot be contacted until June 15th before their junior year of high school. The intention was to eliminate offering scholarships to 7th and 8th graders, but how the new rules will play out and how they will affect recruiting is unclear.

- Increased social media use by program and players: Virtually all programs now use social media to inform and bond with their fans and recruits, and most student-athletes have their own accounts as well. Helping your student-athletes understand the potential benefits as well as pitfalls of social media is crucial. The explosion of video sites such as TikTok expands both opportunities and potential risks. Already, recruits have lost athletic scholarships because of ill-considered posts. Some student-athletes have had to delete their accounts because of abuse heaped upon them by "fans" after a painful loss.

- Enhanced TV coverage of women's athletics: With volleyball's increased presence on broadcast and cable networks, players' and programs' visibility are rising. As Mary Wise, Florida volleyball coach, says:

> "My hope is the next generation coming into college will have grown up watching collegiate women compete on television. They will learn to model their game by watching elite players, just as boys have been able to do for decades."

NCAA SPORTS RADAR SCREEN: INSIDE MOVING OUT

Figure 11-3: Radar screen: inside moving out

Blips on the inside moving out are things that once were once true or relevant but are becoming less so every day. Here is a starter set of current blips for NCAA programs (Most of these examples will be relevant to all sports):

- "Toughen them up" has changed to Data-Driven Care: It used to be thought that training had to be difficult to make the athletes tough. Now training is data-driven to protect the athlete and to accelerate their physical and mental growth.

- Quantity over quality: Before science-based training, the idea was reps, reps, and more reps. Programs still following that approach will experience more repetitive motion injuries than ones who prioritize the quality of training over the quantity of jumps. For example, in the past, Utah volleyball held three sessions of practice a day in preseason camps. Today's science tells us that you will get better results from one or two deliberate practices.

- Scheduling based on proximity vs. scheduling to maximize RPI: RPI is the metric used by the NCAA to rank athletic teams in many sports. Who you schedule is critical for maximizing RPI and thereby improving your rankings for postseason play.

- Coaches being all things to all players: The days are long past when coaches could be all things to their players. Now one of the coach's main roles is leading and managing support services.

- Non-science-based training: The advantages science-based training gives in terms of strength, speed, and protection against injury mean that non-science-based programs will be at a severe disadvantage.

- Qualitative performance analysis: What you think you see may not be true. Quantitative measurements and trend plotting are replacing subjective qualitative performance analysis. Numbers may be misinterpreted, but they don't lie.

- Keeping your job because they like you: Being liked by your boss is a wonderful thing. But in the absence of a winning program, being nice is insufficient to guarantee job security at most institutions.

CREATING YOUR RADAR SCREEN

We encourage you to create your own radar screen with your staff and players. Everyone benefits by thinking of how things are changing, and your players may see things differently than your staff do. Because your players are closer in age to the recruits you are trying to attract, their insights may be different from yours and might prove quite valuable.

After you have identified the blips on the radar screen, spend some time to flesh them out. Think of it like double-clicking on a computer to get the next level of detail within a folder. When you double-click, you develop more detail about why the blip matters and how it will affect you.

You then ask if the blip is good for you or bad for you. If it is good for you, you want the blip to come in strong and fast because it will benefit you. If it is bad for you, you wish it would just go away. If most of the blips are good for you, that is a signal your program is on the right track. If most of the blips are bad for you, the world ahead of you will be more difficult than the world of today.

One thing to keep in mind about the blips on the radar screen is that they are constantly changing. A radar screen from five years ago will feel dated as all of the blips will either have been incorporated into your program or will have faded away. A radar screen exercise should be done periodically to stay current on the changes that will affect your program.

EXAMPLES OF THE NEXT LEVEL OF DETAIL ON YOUR BLIPS

In this section, we will double-click on five blips to illustrate what the next level of detail looks like. For one of the blips (NIL), we will show an analysis that is deeper still to show you what is possible when you really dig into a topic. The blips we will look at more closely are:

- Outside moving in:

    ◦ Name, Image, and Likeness (NIL)

- ° Players bringing in outside leadership concepts
- ° Increased use of the transfer portal

- Inside moving out:

  - ° "Toughen them up" has changed to Data-Driven Care
  - ° Scheduling based on proximity vs. scheduling to maximize RPI.

NAME, IMAGE, AND LIKENESS (NIL)

Name, Image, and Likeness (NIL) is a change that will allow student-athletes to profit by accepting money from their popularity without losing their eligibility or scholarships. It is also a case study in the futility of fighting the radar screen and trying to prevent inevitable changes.

Before NIL, student-athletes were prohibited from profiting from the fame arising from their roles as student-athletes. They could take jobs associated with their sport such as coaching club teams, but could not get paid for making appearances or endorsements.

It was not the case that there was no money to spread around. The athlete's school could freely make money on TV rights, ticket sales, jersey sales, and numerous other items. It was just that not a penny of this money was allowed to flow to student-athletes.

To illustrate the disparity, NCAA Division One football teams have 85 athletic scholarships. Suppose each one is worth $40,000/ year. That would mean there is $3.4 million/year going to the players in scholarships. According to Forbes magazine, there were 31 head football coaches in Division 1 who made more than $4 million/year in 2019. Head coaches make more money than all of their athletes combined, and they can freely supplement their income with endorsements, TV shows, personal appearances, podcasts, etc.

But players were not allowed any supplements above and beyond their scholarships which cover their tuition, room and board and, fairly recently, a cost of living stipend. The stipend is optional, and athletic departments that can afford it can choose to pay for daily essentials such as internet, entertainment, toiletries, cell phones and cell phones service, etc.

People outside the world of athletics would see that as an unfair splitting of the pie. But within athletics, the NCAA took a hard stand against any ability of athletes to profit. In June of 2019, the NCAA said NIL was an existential threat to collegiate athletics and threatened to prohibit California schools from participating in NCAA championships if the state passed a law allowing NIL.

Then in September 2019, California Senate Bill 206 (the Fair Pay to Play Act) passed and gave California student-athletes the right to earn money from their name, image, and likeness. Colorado and Florida followed with similar bills, and several other states have NIL bills in process.

In October of 2019 (less than six months after saying NIL was an existential threat), the NCAA reversed their position with the following statement:

> "In the Association's continuing efforts to support college athletes, the NCAA's top governing board voted unanimously to permit students participating in athletics the opportunity to benefit from the use of their name, image and likeness in a manner consistent with the collegiate model."

It is not difficult to get into the $50,000 a year range for a well-known student-athlete through things like $3,000/month in social media ad revenues, $1,000 for a half hour at a child's birthday party, or $30 a pop for a two-minute personalized video on Cameo.com.

What issues might NIL cause for your program? Perhaps you already experience drama between your stars and your bench players. How will this be magnified when your stars are bringing in $50K/year in NIL money and bench players get naught but scraps? The NCAA insists this won't be connected to recruiting. But what if a local car dealer offers a recruit an endorsement deal? Or, what if it happens at a rival school and they get the recruit you had wanted? If your star player lands an endorsement deal with a local company, will that company reduce their advertising support for your athletic department since they are already paying your star?

The demands on your student-athletes are already enormous. How tempting will it be for them to add paying gigs in addition to all the other demands on their time? What team rules will you install to limit the potential distractions and risks from NIL now that the NCAA has approved the concept?

You might not like Name, Image, and Likeness. You might wish it had never happened. You might think it is a disastrous decision. But like it or not, the NIL blip is coming in hard and fast. Your choice is to either get ahead of the issue and have some control over how it plays out, or fight it and let others determine your fate.

PLAYERS BRINGING OUTSIDE LEADERSHIP CONCEPTS

Players have access to the same books and internet as coaches do, and they can uncover concepts and experts that can contribute to the program. As an example, at Utah the players picked up the book *Legacy* by James Kerr, which tells the story of (arguably) the most successful international athletic team in any sport over the past few decades, the New Zealand All Blacks rugby team.

The players took it upon themselves to define and adopt legacy tasks, as described in the book. These were:

- First years: Take care of the locker room.
- Sophomores: Choose what to wear for different activities.
- Juniors: Understand practice drills and help coaches lead the team.
- Seniors: Assemble a Leadership Council and focus on culture.

They also set their own standards and worked with their coaches to create team goals called Big Rocks. These included their together themes and high-performance (HP) systems and skills:

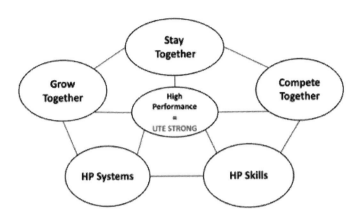

Figure 11-4: Utah volleyball's Big Rocks.

Senior Berkeley Oblad contributed her graphic art talents to develop graphics based on the big rocks:

Figure 11-5: Berkeley Oblad's graphics for the Big Rocks.

By welcoming ideas from the players, the staff leveraged their own time and quickly obtained buy-in since the players had been involved from the beginning.

INCREASED USE OF THE TRANSFER PORTAL

The transfer portal simplifies the process and ensures compliance when a student-athlete transfers from one program to another. The portal does not make transferring a free-for-all since there are still rules, but it makes what was once hard much easier.

This can be a good thing when the player and the program agree they are not a good fit for each other and a parting of the ways is the best course of action for both parties. The reasons a student-athlete might transfer range from tension with the staff or teammates, to lack of playing time, to homesickness and geographical concerns.

The challenge is that the transfer portal provides an easy out, rather than forcing a player to deal with their issues and learn lifelong lessons from doing so. It may be that the poor fit with the program was the root cause of all their problems, and once they transfer, everything will be better. But it also may be that the issues lie within the player and will follow them to the new program.

As Tom Farden, Utah gymnastics coach, said:

> "In the past, some days or even seasons were challenging, but the ability to persevere and chase long-term goals superseded both the coaches' and athletes' desire to look for a 'quick fix.'"

There is another issue with the transfer portal, and that is its effect of transfers on your culture and attitude of your players. How will your current players be affected if a teammate transfers out? And perhaps more importantly, how will they be affected if a player transfers in who jumps ahead of them on the depth chart after they worked hard to secure a starting position?

It used to be that you strived to win with the team you had set and planned on for that year. But with the possibilities afforded by the transfer portal, international players, and graduate transfers, your team is not always fixed. New players can be brought in, which also means that some players might move even further down the depth chart.

The first part of Beth's vision is "Win at the highest level." Bringing in high-level players might help you do this, but doing so might disappoint your existing players who thought they would have the job. This creates a balancing act between the improvement created by the new player and the potential decline in team dynamics caused by frustration and possibly distrust of the coaching staff.

It also raises the issue of what exactly your vision means. Is it "Win at the highest level," or is it "Win at the highest level without disturbing the status quo?" If it is the first, part of your culture must include the primacy of winning even if it means some members of the team may have to sacrifice for the betterment of the team.

Coaching is both and art and a science, and you must look at both sides of the equation as you make your choice of whether or not to bring a new player into the program. We attempted to develop givens you might use for bringing new players onboard, but every time we did it seems you could think of exceptions to the rule and the givens didn't make sense. Because bringing in new players has the potential of causing disruption, it seems this decision falls more on the art side than the science side.

"TOUGHEN THEM UP" HAS CHANGED TO DATA-DRIVEN CARE

Early in Beth's career, the common practice in athletics was on high-intensity, high-quantity training to prepare players for the grueling competition ahead. The thinking was that if the athletes were not pushed past their perceived physical and mental limits, they would become soft and uncompetitive.

Today's data-driven science, however, shows that athletes grow better and faster through application of expertise from sports performance, sports science, athletic training, sports nutrition, and mental health and performance experts. These are the foundations of Utah's Volleyball Performance Team.

As an example of the data-driven approach, all Utah players wear VERT devices, which are about the size of a USB drive, that clip on their shorts and measure the number and height of each of their jumps. The devices connect to an app that enables graphing and analysis of team and individual jumps. Beth has managers track the number of jumps in practice each day and has them alert her if they hit a certain number. She will often stop a player from continuing to jump or will call practice if the jump quantity is getting too high.

After a difficult stretch of matches and training, players began to complain that they had been jumping too much and were feeling fatigued. The analysis using VERT data showed that the actual number of jumps had been going down each practice while the average jump height was still increasing. This showed the taper phase of the periodization plan was working. It also showed the players that there was a good chance their tiredness was more mental than physical.

After being shown the jump data, the players were asked to look at their recent behaviors and look for other reasons they might be feeling tired. How had their eating habits been, and had they had good nutrition to fuel their bodies for the rigors of training? Had they gotten enough sleep? Had they been procrastinating on their academic projects and adding unnecessary stress? Once they identified these other behaviors that had contributed to their fatigue, the players trusted their staff and were able to refocus on their volleyball goals.

SCHEDULING BASED ON PROXIMITY VS. SCHEDULING TO MAXIMIZE RPI

For many years, you would schedule preseason matches with nearby teams that you knew and with whom you had long-standing relationships. The players enjoyed playing against their former high school and club teammates and the fans loved it. This generated a feeling of regional camaraderie and friendly competition. Because you played the same teams time and again, it made for easy travel and simplified planning.

All that changed with the rising importance of the Rating Percentage Index (RPI). RPI is used by the NCAA to rank collegiate volleyball, baseball, softball, hockey, soccer, and lacrosse teams. The RPI ranking for volleyball is determined by your winning percentage (25%), the winning percentage of your opponents (50%), and the winning percentage of the opponents of your opponents (25%).

This places a heavy emphasis on the strength of your schedule. If you schedule and defeat weak opponents, it does little to help your RPI unless they schedule and defeat even weaker opponents. Scheduling becomes strategic as you examine which teams you should add and what effects defeating them would have on your RPI.

Some criticize RPI because it weights a victory on the road the same as one at home, when it seems a road victory should be more impressive. Others criticize RPI because you can beat an inferior team that piles up wins in a weak conference and it counts the same as beating a top team that has the same number of wins playing against higher-ranked opponents.

The RPI calculation doesn't take into account how strong or weak your opponents are; you are in essence just trying to capture their wins. For these reasons, NCAA basketball stopped using RPI in 2018 in favor of the NET metric, which includes a much broader range of inputs. But for now, NCAA volleyball rankings are still determined using RPI.

Whether you agree with the RPI or not, it is what is used to determine bids, seedings, and host sites for the NCAA tournament. That means you must schedule to maximize RPI, and that may force you to break up traditional local rivalries. The focus on RPI changes the idea from "You have to play the best to be the best" to "You have to selectively choose opponents to assure victory and absorb their wins to bolster your RPI to be the best."

ARE YOU PREPARED FOR THE FUTURE OR STUCK IN THE PAST?

The radar screen is a tool that looks at external factors and how they might affect your program. It describes how the world around you is changing, but it says nothing about your program. The next step is to evaluate how well your program matches where the world is headed.

Think of all the different parts of your program. A good place to start is the detailed above-the-line topic list from the leadership agenda tool in Chapter 4. You might want to break large items such as recruiting down into their 10–15 component parts. Once you have done this, create a table with two columns:

Better positioned for the world of three years ago	Well positioned for the world of three years from now
•	•
•	•
•	•
•	•

Figure 11-6: Radar screen positioning template

Now go through each part of your program. If a part of the program is well aligned with where the radar screen is going, place it in the right-hand column. If it is feeling stale or is not consistent with the radar screen, place it in the left-hand column. Once you have categorized each part of your program you will have a visual representation of which parts are prepared for the future and which parts are stuck in the past.

As an example from outside the world of athletics, think of Sears. Sears went bankrupt in 2019 and closed hundreds of stores. How did this diminish your life? For most of you, the answer is, almost assuredly, not at all. Sears had become irrelevant. Other stores were cheaper. Or had better merchandise. Or had better customer service. Sears was living in the past, and people had simply stopped thinking of them.

People typically worry about making mistakes and taking actions that go wrong. But that isn't the real danger your program faces. You can recover from mistakes, and some of the things you try will turn out great. The real danger your program faces is moving too slowly and becoming irrelevant because people stop thinking of you.

This is the danger your program faces if you have too many parts on the left-hand side. Recruits will stop thinking about you because other programs feel fresher and more up-to-date. Recruiting will decline, leading to a worse record, leading to fewer fans, leading to worse recruiting, and the vicious cycle will build on itself.

FOR WHICH YEAR ARE YOU DESIGNED TO COMPETE?

From the exercise above, take a look at the parts of your program that are ready for the future and those which are stuck in the past. If they were all equally important, and you had the same number of items on each side, then on average you would be designed to compete today. If you have more parts (or more important parts) on the right-hand side, you would be designed to compete in the future. If you have more parts (or more important parts) on the left-hand side, you would be designed for a prior era.

Some companies and programs are designed to win in the future, and some are better matched for competing in the past and the world as it was. For example, Tesla appears to be 3–4 years ahead of other automobile companies when it comes to electric cars. They are designed to win in the future.

On the other hand, consider the Yellow Pages. What is the very first thing you do when the Yellow Pages is dropped off at the end of your driveway? If you did not immediately answer "toss it in the recycling," you are in the minority. It turns out that carrying around a bulky, out-of-date, impossible to search subset of the internet filled with advertisements is less attractive than it once was.

Weighing the parts of your program that are ready for the future, the parts that are stuck in the past, and the relative importance of each part, ask yourself this:

For which year is your program designed to compete?

HOW FAST ARE YOU CHANGING?

How fast are you changing relative to the broader world around you? If you ask only one question to test the health of your program, this might be it.

If you are changing faster than the world around you, you will be out in front. You will make mistakes, but you will have time to recover from them. If you are changing at the same rate as the world around you, at least you are not falling behind.

The danger sign is if you are changing more slowly than the world around you. If that is the case, you will lose more and more relevance each year. You may be changing slowly because you want to avoid mistakes or because you simply don't like to change.

Sometimes, however, resistance to change is caused by the legacy of past success. As Terry Pettit, former Nebraska volleyball coach, said:

"The more success a coach has, the harder it is to have the motivation to change."

ARE YOU DESIGNED TO WIN
IN THE COMING YEARS?

The radar screen tells you how the world is changing around you. You can separate your program into the parts that are ready for the future, as shown by the radar screen, and those that are stuck in the past. You can estimate the year in which you are designed to compete. Finally, you can compare the rate of change of your program to that of the world around you.

If the year you are designed to compete in is this year or even later, and you are changing faster than the world around you, congratulations. You are in the sweet spot and most likely are designed to win.

On the other hand, if you are designed to compete in an earlier year, and you change more slowly than the world around you, each year that passes sets your program farther behind. This is the path to irrelevance and failure.

MAIN POINTS IN THIS CHAPTER

- The radar screen describes how the world is changing around you.
- Parts of your program are ready for the future, and other parts are stuck in the past.
- Identifying the trends going on around you enables you to identify necessary changes to keep your program relevant.
- Your program's rate of change is critical to its success.

CHAPTER 12: LEADERSHIP TIES EVERYTHING TOGETHER

"Management is a set of processes that can keep a complicated system of people and technology running smoothly...Leadership defines what the future should look like, aligns people with that vision, and inspires them to make it happen despite the obstacles."

John Kotter (Professor of Leadership, Emeritus, Harvard Business School)

COACHING IS BOTH AN ART AND A SCIENCE

Coaching in particular, and leadership in general, are both an art and a science. The science side will tell you what the best practices are and what you are supposed to do. The art side harnesses your creativity to deviate from general rules to address the specific situations in which you find yourself.

As an example, Utah has the unusual case of having their two best hitters both being left-handed. The science side (statistical data) says that when a left-handed hitter plays in the opposite position and hits from the right side, they hit for a higher percentage. The ball does not have to travel across their body, and this reduces complexity and enhances repeatability.

However, for a left-side or outside hitter, being right-handed is the norm and has the same advantage as a left-handed player who is hitting on the right. Another disadvantage of a lefty on the left side is the difficulty of hitting an out-of-system set when the passing breaks down. When the set is coming from deep in the court, it makes it even more of a challenge for a left-hander to deal with the difficult angle.

If Beth followed the science and did what was normal, she would have most likely put both lefties as opposite hitters on the right side and run a 6-2 offense. This would have meant both players would have to come off the court for a setter to take their place, thus reducing both players' time on the court.

To keep both of her best hitters on the court full time, Beth moved one of the lefties to the outside hitter spot on the left side in January and never looked back. By playing one player out of their normal position, she would have the best players on court for as much of the time as possible, and that would increase her probability of winning.

It took a lot of work to get the lefty on the outside to understand the position and its different angles. But with her being one of the top athletes in the program, it was worth taking the risk. Moving her also reduced potential tensions since both lefties knew they deserved maximum playing time and would have been frustrated if they were not getting it. And since both lefties were named All-Americans, Beth's creativity in the art of volleyball seems to have paid off.

THE NEED FOR BOTH LEADERSHIP AND MANAGEMENT

Much of this book describes how to manage your program. We have provided tools and concepts for getting the right work done, by the right people, and for assuring alignment at all levels of the organization. Beth describes this as having the right people in the right seats on the bus.

Management without leadership creates efficiency but not effectiveness. Management describes how to get the day-to-day work done within the existing system under the existing rules. It is leadership that allows you to change the system and/or create new rules.

If you follow the path of management without leadership, it will inevitably result in a program that is simply competing hard. Everyone will be doing their best, but they will be doing so within a program which may or may not be designed to win. To be fully designed to win, you must have both leadership and management so you are playing the right game and doing so in the right way.

Earlier in this book, we quoted the characteristics of a leader as described by Jay Lund, CEO of Andersen Corporation:

- Deep understanding of the business.
- Vision.
- Inspired leadership.
- Courage and resiliency.
- Data-driven with an ability to connect the dots.

- Conviction balanced with judgment, objectivity, and humility.
- Results-driven.

We will use this outline to address leadership and its vital role in being designed to win.

DEEP UNDERSTANDING OF THE BUSINESS

We could have changed this to "Deep Understanding of the Sport," but you need mastery of both the athletic and business sides of your sport. In large part, this is what this book has been about.

Young coaches know they need to learn the details of their sports and the tips and tricks for becoming a great coach: The X's and O's. They were most likely athletes themselves and have an appreciation of the intensity of competition and the passion for winning. They understand athletics from the players' perspective, which is a great place to start.

But your education cannot end there. If all you can do is coach on the field or court, you will run into problems with budgeting, delegation, marketing, cross-functional teams, academics, administrative support, compliance, and a host of other topics including, but not limited to, team dynamics, mental performance, and leadership development. In summary, you will not have clarity and alignment within your program.

You can't take the time to become an expert on all of these topics, but you must earn your right to coach by developing an appreciation for them and the ability to oversee them all at a minimally acceptable level. If you don't, they will create problems that will bring you headaches and distract you from recruiting and developing your players and team. You want to address these issues so you can get back to coaching, which, if you remember, was the reason you entered the field in the first place.

DEEP UNDERSTANDING OF THE SPORT

Mary Wise, Florida volleyball coach, described the importance of a deep understanding of all aspects of your sport in this way:

> "Simply competing hard is actually easier. If you do that, you can just show up on game day and compete. Being designed to win means you have a 360-degree understanding and approach that affects all aspects of performance (recruiting, training, match prep, character development, staff competencies, etc.)"

Understanding their sport is where many coaches focus their efforts, and rightfully so. We haven't covered much on the pure coaching side in this book, however, because there is already abundant information and knowledge in this area that is readily available to young coaches.

To build your understanding of your sport, you can do the following:

- Network with more experienced coaches and those that have a different perspective from the program at which you are currently employed. Two of the best venues for networking are at age-group tournaments in which coaches line the sidelines watching their prospects and at numerous coaching conventions held in conjunction with their sport's National Championship.
- Attend local and national in-person coaching clinics.

- Access online learning sites. They have a plethora of content including video of the correct ways to play and coach the game.
- Reach out to a coach you respect and ask to spend a week in their gym.
- Read memoirs of the legendary coaches who have come before you. Most coaching books are filled with anecdotes and stories from the careers of those at the top of the field. When you read these books, search for similarities with the situations you have faced and ask yourself which of their solutions might work for you.
- Read books from outside your sport that are relevant to learning, competition, and leadership. The examples will be from different fields, but the ideas and approaches can be adapted to the situations you face.

VISION AS A HEAD COACH

Early in the book, we presented Beth's three-part vision for her volleyball program:

- Win at the highest level.
- Learn lifelong lessons and become a lifelong learner.
- Have a team that loves, trusts, and respects each other.

Beth's vision may be refined over time, but it will not be fundamentally changed. Because she has led the Utah program for more than 30 years, her vision has become the Utah program's vision.

Every coach must develop their own philosophy and coaching vision. Your vision is an expression of your deeply held set of personal beliefs about how things should be done, and it will guide you throughout your career. The exercises of putting it in writing and then expanding or narrowing your vision year after year will lead to a clear and concise statement that will make all of your choices easier.

USING VISION IN RECRUITING YOUR STAFF

Your vision can be a powerful recruiting tool for both players and staff. At the entry level, people are eager to break into coaching, and will take almost any job to get their foot in the door. As their career grows and matures, however, they will seek alignment between their own developing view of how a program should be run and the vision of your program.

People are attracted to those who have a clear view of what they want. Even if that view does not perfectly match their own, it feels comforting to join a team run by someone who can state their beliefs and who can back them up with processes, procedures, and practices that are aligned with what they believe. Clarity of vision also attracts recruits and their families who can visualize the experience ahead of them more clearly when the program's vision is crisp and compelling.

VISION AS AN ASSISTANT COACH

If you are an assistant coach, you can influence your program's vision by bringing ideas, raising issues, and making suggestions. In fact, part of your role is to test the boundaries of what is acceptable. But it is also your role to accept the program's vision as a source of givens and to make decisions and take actions aligned with those givens.

For example, suppose you believed your role is to coach the mechanics and systems of volleyball and felt nothing else was more important. When you become a head coach someday, you can instill that vision in your program. But if you were working under Beth, your personal vision would not align with her vision of "Learn lifelong lessons and become a lifelong learner." Either you would have to place your vision on the back burner and support Beth's, or your lack of alignment would generate conflict after conflict.

THE VISION OF A BIG HAIRY AUDACIOUS GOAL (BHAG)

Sometimes a program needs to be shaken up. James Collins and Jerry Porras, in their book *Built to Last: Successful Habits of Visionary Companies*, introduced the concept of the Big Hairy Audacious Goal, or BHAG. This is something far beyond a typical vision. A BHAG is a target so radical that it shocks someone to even say it out loud.

Should your program need to be shaken up, the approach of setting and aligning behind a BHAG might be a good way to do it. Because it is so much more aggressive than a typical goal of doing a bit better than last year, a BHAG forces you to rethink everything contributing to the success of your program.

This is the mindset Beth adopted when Utah entered the Pac-12. Simply improving around the edges would not have been enough to move Utah from the bottom third of the conference to the top third. It took audacity to target the top third of the conference and to develop an action plan to consistently beat the national powerhouse programs to make it happen. Having realized her BHAG, the goals of Beth's program have now progressed to winning the conference and the national championship.

The renaissance genius Michelangelo put it this way:

"The greater danger for most of us lies not in setting our aim too high and falling short; but in setting our aim too low, and achieving our mark."

CREATING YOUR VISION REQUIRES BIG BLOCKS OF TIME

There is a special kind of magic that arises from big blocks of time. In eight one-hour sessions, you waste much of your time reminding people where you were at the end of your last session before getting started on the current session. In one eight-hour session, however, you get can get deep into the topic and accelerate your progress.

For example, to prepare for the first of the one-hour talks we gave for the American Volleyball Coaches Association, Leo and Beth blocked out a full day. We spent the morning discussing the ideas and points we wanted to include. This continued over a walk and lunch, and the afternoon was spent turning the ideas into draft slides. We worked separately on refining the slides for a week and then met for another half day to discuss the changes. After another week working separately, we met for two hours to finalize the presentation. Had we tried to do this work one hour at a time, we might never have completed the initial presentation that led to this book.

As another example, a single sheet of paper showed Leo that one of his best clients understood the need for creativity, freedom, and big blocks of time to develop a winning vision. To get on the agenda of a strategic leadership team (normally the CEO and their seven direct reports), people compete for 30-minute blocks. They must clearly define the topic they will be discussing, provide their slides in advance, and stay within the bounds of their approved subject. When you see the printed agenda, it uses small print to describe exactly what will happen so that there are no surprises during the day.

The one-page agenda for a leadership retreat Leo was involved in started off with five topics before lunch on the first day, all neatly and completely described. These were defined business items, and they had to be taken care of quickly and efficiently.

After lunch, and for all the next day, the agenda just said "Leo." There was no description and no specific topic. Leo had a number of tools and exercises in mind, but developing the vision required going where the conversation needed to go. It could not be predicted or forced; it had to be allowed to flow and find its own form.

VISION REQUIRES LEADERSHIP COMMITMENT

Business leaders spend most of their time reviewing the work of others. The role of the CEO is to guide the work of their teams and to make decisions based on their recommendations.

But there are some topics that can't be delegated and that require active engagement by the leader. Tres Lund is the CEO of Lund Food Holdings, which runs 27 high-end grocery stores in Minneapolis and St. Paul. Lund wanted a clear vision for how he could remain relevant with all of the changes going on in the grocery industry such as meal kits, new checkout technologies, and the demand for local and natural food.

Lund formed a working team that spent two days a month with Leo for an entire year. Rather than having the members of this team simply report to him with their recommendations at the end of the effort, Lund assigned himself to the team. He rolled up his sleeves as an equal participant and analyzed the business from every perspective. When the effort concluded, Lund did not have to be convinced that the team had done a good job. He already understood the quality of the work since he had been an active participant.

The only way Lund could have invested as much time as he did was because he is a grandmaster at delegation. He follows the golden rule and delegates everything that can be delegated. That leaves him with big blocks of time to invest in the small number of things that truly matter. He never knows what might come up and require his time, but he knows there will always be something. That knowledge enables him to say "No." to tasks even before he knows the projects to which he will be saying "Yes!"

THE IMPORTANCE OF INSPIRED LEADERSHIP

To be a leader, you need people who feel inspired to follow you. Being an inspirational leader is less about the contribution you make through your own work and more about the effect your leadership has on others.

Inspired leaders make the people around them better. They help them see how they can become the best version of themselves and give them the guidance and tools they need to improve. This doesn't mean the leader is trying to clone themselves by forcing their staff into their own mold. It means that the leader understands and appreciates the differences between individuals and recognizes that the best version of each staff member may be very different from the path they themselves have taken.

Inspired leaders display their passion and make it safe for their staff to do so as well. It is nearly impossible to convince your staff that they should be passionate if you are not setting the example. The more intense your passion, the more they will want it for themselves.

Amy Hogue, University of Utah softball head coach, highlighted the importance of inspiring everyone when she said:

> "Too often, coaches feel as though they are the ones driving team culture and putting in the effort to create and maintain a great team culture. And while it's important for accountability and organization to start at the top, it's just as important for the team to drive the continuity of standards."

THE POWER OF EMPATHETIC LEADERSHIP

One of the most important characteristics you need to develop is empathy with your staff and players. Leading requires that you care for your people and that you get to know who they are as individuals, understand what is important to them, and learn about what they are willing to share with you regarding what is happening in their lives.

Empathy can't be faked. It is not just about memorizing facts about people's lives. It is about building active listening skills and genuinely taking an interest in others and seeing the world from their perspectives. To some, this comes naturally. To others, it is a muscle that must be used to grow strong.

Empathy is also important for working in a diverse world. If you can't put yourself in the shoes of those who are different than you, you will tend to hire and recruit people with the same backgrounds, ethnicities, religious and political beliefs, genders, and sexual preference as yourself. By doing so, you will have more comfort and ease in communicating, since they will share many of your views, but you will lose out on talented contributors simply because they do not share your background and experiences.

COURAGE AND WILLINGNESS TO TAKE RISKS

Courage and willingness to take risks are necessary aspects of leadership. If you want a high RPI, you need to schedule strong teams, some of whom will beat you. If you can't accept this, you will schedule easier teams and that will place a limit on how high your RPI can go. Other examples of courage include:

- Being willing to change your lineup even when you are winning because you believe it is necessary to reach your team's full potential.
- Disciplining a player for long-term benefit even when you know it will cause short-term resentment.
- Being able to dig deep and search for answers on Monday morning after two tough losses over the weekend.
- Saying "No!" to something that would greatly help your program but which doesn't align with your vision and values.

Karch Kiraly, USA women's national volleyball team coach, told us:

> "I don't want my tombstone to say: 'Here lies Karch, he played it safe.'"

RESILIENCY IS CRITICAL FOR LEADERSHIP

Resiliency is a requirement of leadership because there will inevitably be setbacks. You may have injuries, you may lose out on a top recruit, or your budget may be cut. You won't necessarily know what is coming at you, but there will always be something.

Part of leadership is helping your staff deal with failure. If your staff doesn't fail, they are not trying hard enough and you are not pushing them to their limits. When they do fail, your response will dictate what happens the next time they go all out. If you let them know you have failed in the past and that it is a natural part of growth, they will feel supported and confident enough to try again.

If you come down hard on them, they will give up on the folly of trying things they are not sure they can do and fall back to what is safe and which will almost assuredly work. You will have placed a hard ceiling on their growth and ensured they will view success as not making mistakes rather than becoming the best they can be. In the lyrics of "Tubthumping" by the British rock band Chumbawamba:

> "I get knocked down, but I get up again. You are never going to keep me down."

Or in the words of Winston Churchill:

> "Never give in, never give in, never, never, never, never—in nothing, great or small, large or petty—never give in except to convictions of honour and good sense."

CLAIMING YOUR PLACE AT THE TABLE

When Beth first entered the Pac-12, she would attend club tournaments in search of players to recruit to the highly competitive new conference. As she walked around the convention centers, she would see her new colleagues doing the same thing. It is human nature that you feel slightly intimidated when you see coaches that you have respected, that have won national championships, and are now your peers in the Pac-12. But if you don't believe you are their equal and deserving of their respect, why should they?

Beth developed a habit of searching out the biggest names and most distinguished coaches she could find at the court she was watching. She would wait until the seat next to them opened up and would sit down and have a conversation with them. Most coaches were intimidated by the big names, and it was surprisingly easy to find empty seats next to them.

This took courage, but it established her as a peer amongst the top coaches in the sport, both in the Pac-12 and nationally, and recruits noticed this. It also formed the core of her network as she would speak with them again and again at tournaments and at the American Volleyball Coaching Association convention. The people she sat next to now make up both her professional network and her long-time friends.

By positioning herself as an equal with the coaches she respected, it became easier for herself and for others to see her as belonging in the elite group she found herself in as a head coach in the Pac-12. Now, Beth is the coach at tournaments with the empty seat next to her. Will you be the next one to sit down and introduce yourself?

DATA-DRIVEN WITH AN ABILITY
TO CONNECT THE DOTS

Sports analytics was popularized in the book and movie *Money-ball*, which told the story of a major league baseball team that used Sabermetrics (advanced data analytics) to create competitive advantage. The 2002 Oakland Athletics had little talent and a limited ability to attract star players, but they had a person in the program that understood the importance of data analytics. They used massive amounts of data to determine with confidence the attributes that led directly to winning.

For example, they found that on-base percentage contributes more to winning than does runs batted in. They used this knowledge to target draft picks and free agents who excelled at their analytical criteria but who were undervalued by other teams. Though the A's did not win the World Series as portrayed in the movie, data analytics did indeed turn their franchise around.

Statistics tell a story but can be dangerous if your data are incomplete or improperly interpreted. Each data point is a snapshot, a view at a single moment in time. That point tells you what is happening now, not what has been happening in the past or what might happen in the future. But by analyzing changes in data over time, you will observe the underlying trends and build insight into what is actually occurring.

REGRESSION TO THE MEAN

Regression to the mean states that if you have an extreme result, it is likely to be an outlier. The next result will most likely be closer to the historical average. This is true both for extremely good and extremely bad results. The goal is to improve the mean over time.

If a player has a peak performance one day, it does not mean they will repeat that level of performance the next day. In fact, they will tend to regress to their normal skill level. Reacting to one peak performance and expecting it to happen every time will leave you disappointed.

The opposite is true as well. If a player has a bad day, reacting to that single day could lead to lasting negative results such as loss of confidence or unnecessarily trying to fix something that is not broken. By understanding that a player will regress to the mean, you can have confidence they will perform at the level you expect the following day.

This concept can distort the athlete's perception of their performance. If they do not understand regression to the mean, they may be too confident in their abilities after a peak performance or too down on themselves after a bad day. The true story lies in the upward or downward trends. When you understand the stories the data are trying to tell you, you will become a more effective coach and leader.

CONVICTION BALANCED WITH JUDGMENT, OBJECTIVITY, AND HUMILITY

Smart people, once they think they are right, become dumb people. They tune out input from others, and when they have a conversation, they are not listening to what the other person is saying. Instead, as they pretend to listen, they are really planning their rebuttal, so they can prove they were correct.

You need heartfelt beliefs and powerful commitment to lead your program. But your beliefs must be tempered by the fact that you don't know every last thing and you may be able to improve what you are doing by really listening and benefitting from the ideas of others. Doing so requires humility and reaching out to others rather than feeling the need to always provide the answers yourself.

You are not a failure if others find ways to improve your work. The failure would be in not taking the opportunity to improve your work because it is too difficult to admit to yourself and others that your brilliant idea wasn't perfect the first time you let others hear about it. Be grateful for the gift of ideas from others that refine and improve upon your own ideas.

PROGRAM PARTNERS BRING IDEAS FROM OUTSIDE OF YOUR SPORT

You are limited by NCAA rules on how many assistants you can have, and budget limitations place additional constraints on your program. But there are underutilized assets sitting right in front of you, and those are your fans.

Just as not all fans will be donors, not all fans will have capabilities and experience your program needs. But some will. The challenge is to identify who can help and in which areas you would like to ask for their assistance. You and your staff have limited time, so if you bring someone in, they must be ready to contribute with minimal direction. That means they should be well established in their field so they have something valuable to offer, and can do so without wasting your time or causing distractions.

The partnering we are talking about is at a different level than simply hiring a consultant. Consultants help with specific areas of your program for which they have expertise. Programs hire consultants every day to perform tasks given them by the coaching staff. In many cases, the consultants are doing what the staff could do themselves if they had more time.

But a program partner is different. They don't just allow you to offload work from your staff. They bring skills, ideas, tools, and expertise that neither you nor your staff have and that you could never afford to purchase. Most program partners have had successful careers in which they have made enough money that they may be willing to work with you for free or for a discounted rate of which their clients could only dream.

Leo is a program partner with Utah volleyball. He brings ideas and tools from outside the world of sport and works with Beth to see what can be adapted to help her program and what does not fit and should be discarded. Other program partners include a physician who has given talks on remaining healthy and a senior leader at the University who has contributed ideas on leadership in general and on woman's empowerment in particular.

PROGRAM PARTNER RELATIONSHIPS MUST BE DIRECTED BY THE COACH

The people you bring in as partners will be experienced and will not be used to taking orders, but having them do so is absolutely fundamental to making the arrangement work. The relationship must be driven by the coach and the needs of the program. The last thing a coach needs is a wild card from outside causing drama and confusion within the program's boundaries.

Anyone you bring inside the tent must:

- Understand and respect the vision and values of your

program. The more closely they are aligned with your vision, the better.

- Be invested in your program's long-term success. True program partnerships will last for years and go through multiple recruiting classes.
- Possess skills, knowledge, and experience that can be applied to your sport but which are not typically known within it. Consultants you hire know things inside your sport. Program partners know things outside of your sport that can be adapted and made relevant to your program.
- Produce an attractive return on the time a coach must invest to work with the partner.

TRUST IS ESSENTIAL IN YOUR PROGRAM PARTNERS

One of the keys to bringing on a program partner is trust. If you try to take the time to understand all that your partner is going to do, it will never work. If you go down this route, you will need to spend huge amounts of time with the partner so they can educate you on the background, concepts, history, application, hurdles, keys to success, etc. You can't afford to take this time away from your staff and players and still have at least a sliver of time left for your own life.

This means that if you bring someone in as a program partner, you will need to take a chance on their content and how they will tailor their expertise to the situation you are facing. That means you better have worked with them enough times and for a long enough period that you trust them to help your program rather than creating problems for it.

In Chapter 2, we described Leo's talk to the players using the imagery of how Utah started out as the field mice hiding from the predators, but have now transformed into the red-tailed hawks whom the others must fear. But what we didn't tell you was how that talk was developed.

All the guidance Beth gave Leo before the talk was that the team felt lost. That was not terribly specific, and it didn't immediately tell Leo what he should talk about. Leo had never done a motivational speech for an athletic team before, and he sought out more direction from Beth. When he did, she gave the best possible answer—"Leo, I trust you with my team."

From that moment, the weight was on Leo's shoulders to come up with something that would deeply connect with the team and get them refocused on winning. He has given hundreds of keynote speeches, but for those he usually has a topic and prepared ideas. Here, he was starting from scratch.

Seldom has Leo worked as hard on a speech as he did for this one. Once Beth said she trusted him with her team, he was totally committed to putting in whatever work was necessary to come up with something useful that would get through to the players. That is what you want in a partner. You want someone who is committed to your program, wants to help, and feels the pressure not to disappoint and leave things worse off after their contribution.

Beth could never have asked Leo to give this talk if they had not already worked closely together many times and on many different topics. Trust takes time to build and requires interactions of many different kinds to reach the level at which you are ready to bring someone in as a program partner.

RESULTS-DRIVEN AND MEASURING PROGRESS TOWARDS WINNING

Athletics has the ultimate measurement of success in win/loss records. It doesn't matter if you talk a big game. It doesn't matter if you have excuses or rationales. In the end, you have to face the numbers. In particular, your conference record is as close to an apples-to-apples comparison as you can get since you are comparing records with other programs who have played the same teams.

There are other metrics that measure your progress towards winning. These include:

- Are your statistics improving?
- Are the players responding to coaching? Do they have a growth mindset and are they making changes?
- Is the team working hard but just not getting the results... yet?
- Are your staff and the team engaged with the process?
- Is the team doing well academically?
- Is the team representing themselves, the program, and the university well?

If you are not yet getting the bottom-line results you want, keep the focus on the process. The key is to keep your players engaged and hungry to improve even when they are not yet seeing the bottom-line results. With time and patience, the results will come.

INTERNAL LEADERSHIP—FIGHTING YOUR PERSONAL DRAGON

Everyone has a personal dragon they must fight, and the fight requires internal rather than external leadership. The dragon will be with you for years and decades, if not your entire life. Sometimes it will be active, and other times it will be at rest.

Your dragon might be physical, mental, or emotional. It might be rational, tangible, and real, or it may exist solely inside your own mind. Others may think they understand what you are going through and offer to help, but fighting your dragon eventually comes down to a battle of it vs. you.

Dragons are intensely personal, and it is not easy to be open about them. Because of this, people feel they are alone in suffering from something that doesn't seem to bother anyone else. Your dragon is yours alone, but others have beasts of the same breed. When you open yourself up, you will make connections you had not anticipated and will come to realize you are not the only one who fights a secret battle.

Dragons are different from setbacks. During your life you will experience many setbacks. You will have breakups with romantic partners, you will get your knee replaced, you will lose your job, a pet will pass on, you will get into a financial bind. Dealing with these will be terrible and painful, but for setbacks of this type, time will heal all wounds. One, two, or three years after the event, you will have moved on and only the memory will remain.

But dragons stick around. To fight your dragon you will gather information, develop alternatives, try solutions, evaluate the results, and, when things don't work, you will try something else. Perhaps one day you will land on a solution that works and you can shift your focus to continuous improvement. Or perhaps you never reach this stage and either accept defeat or keep trying in the hope that something will finally work. Note that we have talked about fighting your dragon, not slaying it. You can beat it down, but it will never die.

We will each share our personal dragon and will do so in the first person. These are our stories. Yours will be different, but perhaps there are some parts of our stories to which you can relate.

LEO'S DRAGON: NERVES AND STAGE FRIGHT

My professional career was threatened by my inability to deal with nerves and stage fright. Since my job included teaching roomfuls of dozens of people and making speeches to ballrooms filled with hundreds of people, this was a problem I could not avoid. And it would not go away.

I had the complete package—sweating, shortness of breath, strained voice, trembling hands, and dry mouth. My problem grew until I would be more focused on how to deal with my nerves than with the content I was presenting. It finally reached a point where I knew I would either need to learn to control my nerves or find a profession I could do from behind the scenes instead of in front of a crowd.

I understood the problem was not rational. It wasn't as if I had had bad experiences in front of crowds. Overall, I had received good receptions from my audiences, and most would not have guessed the difficulty I had in getting in front of them. I tend to look at the world quite rationally, and it was especially upsetting to know there wasn't a reason or explanation for my nerves. They were just there and wouldn't go away.

I bought two dozen books on dealing with stage fright and read them all. I tried what the books recommended, and it helped a little bit just to know I was facing my fear, but the standard fixes didn't cure my problem. I tried deep breathing, reminded myself that my audience wanted to hear what I had to say, practiced my talks ahead of time, focused on a small number of people in the audience rather than the entire crowd, and realized the worst thing that could happen wasn't all that bad. But the nerves remained.

People would advise me to calm down. That turns out to be well-intentioned but terrible advice. If you are nervous, you are sweating, your heart is pounding, and you are shaking. That is 180 degrees away from being calm with gentle breathing and a slow heart rate. There is just no way to easily transition from nervous to calm. They are emotionally and physically miles apart.

I finally learned of a breakthrough idea that helped me in this fight. Alison Brooks of the Harvard Business School suggests that rather than trying to go from nervous to calm, go from nervous to excited instead. Nervousness and excitement are both high-arousal emotions and share many of the same physical effects. So now when I go on stage, I am not nervous, I am excited.

Other things that have helped me in my battle with nerves:

- Before each of my talks I go into the restroom, look into the mirror, smile, and say "You've got this! You know the material, and they want to hear it." For reasons I don't understand, this releases pent-up tension.

- I plan a pause 45 seconds into every talk. I know I can do 45 seconds even if I feel myself tightening up. At the 45-second mark, I toss a question out to the audience and wait 15 seconds for them to consider their answer. This pause gives me the chance I need to breathe and reset.

At 10 years into my career, I thought I would have to switch to a different field because of my nerves. At 20 years in, I had learned to manage my nerves to an acceptable level. At 30 years in, the nerves are still there, but now they serve to focus me more than to fight against me.

BETH'S DRAGON: CROHN'S DISEASE

I would normally just manage the pain. But, after a long weekend of recruiting, I couldn't take it anymore. I was heading to the emergency room once again.

I was diagnosed with Crohn's disease when I was a junior in high school. Crohn's is an autoimmune disease, which, as described by the Crohn's and Colitis Foundation, "belongs to a group of conditions known as inflammatory bowel diseases (IBD). Crohn's disease is a chronic inflammatory condition of the gastrointestinal tract." Eventually, Crohn's patients end up having sections of their intestines removed because of scar tissue and blockage. I had finally succumbed to the disease and had eight inches of my intestine removed in 2017.

The coaching profession demands long, hard hours, extensive travel, recruiting weekends of 10-hour days, and the constant pressure to win. The profession is tough enough without having a disease that can be debilitating at times. I have never missed a match for this disease, but I was sick a number of times during matches, and very sick after matches. I've had over ten trips to the emergency room including in Oakland, California, after playing Stanford and before a match vs. California Berkeley. I coached the Cal match after convincing the emergency room doctor to release me so I could get back the hotel to be with my team.

I am finally learning the importance of balance. I focus on working out, healthy nutrition, proper hydration, stress management, and mental health to help deal with my chronic illness. By prioritizing these in my life, I have become a better coach. I see many young coaches look stressed out, exhausted, and unhealthy. It's tough to eat well and exercise while on the road or when busily running around at home. But it is so important.

Coaches think they have to give everything to their team, and that they have to give the same to their families and loved ones. In the end though, coaches need to take care of themselves if they are going to be effective leaders of successful programs.

I decided to go public with my health issues when Lee Feinswog from Volleyball Magazine reached out to me. He had heard about my surgery and he wanted to write an article about living with Crohn's as an NCAA Division 1 Head Coach. Some people asked me if I was worried it would affect my recruiting in a negative way. That concern never crossed my mind. When I did the interview with Lee, I knew I wanted the importance of physical and mental health for all coaches, but especially young coaches, to be the take away, and that message came across in the article. It was another way for me to give back to the profession.

Since then, the best thing to happen was that three young coaches who have Crohn's disease contacted me after reading the article. They told me it helped to learn of a coach that has been in the profession for a while with the same issue, and it gave them hope that they too could have a long and fulfilling coaching career.

There is value in sharing in our profession. While it may not lead directly to winning, I believe in karma and that things come around to those that take the opposite approach of trying to win at all costs. Giving back to your sport will help your program tenfold by giving it a richness above and beyond your win/loss record.

PEOPLE LOOK TO LEADERS FOR CONFIDENCE

Leadership is what elevates a well-run program to the next level of success. Even when you are feeling insecure and uncertain, as a leader you must exude confidence and stability

Jay Debertin, CEO of CHS, says that as a leader you have to send the signal that you know how to help the organization work through difficult issues. You must keep an outward appearance that projects confidence while at the same time avoiding arrogance. Even when you are feeling vulnerable and don't have all the answers, you need to show that you have confidence that if we all work together, we can make it through challenging times.

He summed up his approach as follows:

> "If you feel the need to do so, go into the restroom and splash some cold water on your face. You can't go out and have people seeing you looking scared. You've got to put your game-face on."

MAIN POINTS IN THIS CHAPTER

- Coaching is both an art and a science.
- Leaders have a clear vision that guides their decisions and actions.
- Crafting your vision is best done using big blocks of time.
- You need to claim your place at the table as a leader.
- Data and connecting the dots are becoming increasingly necessary for excellent leadership.
- Everyone has a personal dragon, and fighting it requires internal leadership.

CHAPTER 13: SUMMARY AND HOW TO GET STARTED

"Do what you feel in your heart to be right—for you'll be criticized anyway."

Eleanor Roosevelt (longest-serving First Lady of the United States)

In this final chapter, we will give our view as to the differences between athletics and business, our reflections on writing this book, a brief summary of the main points of each chapter, and then finish with our thoughts on how you can get started applying the concepts and tools to your own program.

THE DIFFERENCES BETWEEN SPORTS AND BUSINESS

In this book, we have looked at the intersection of sports and business and found overlaps and similarities that were both important and numerous. But we also found things that really are fundamentally different between the two worlds. Among these are the following:

- In college athletics there is a short time between when you start training an athlete and when they graduate and move on. Collegiate student-athletes typically have four years of eligibility (which they can stretch over a maximum of five years by redshirting and sitting out a year). Though there are few jobs-for-life any longer in business, it is certainly common to spend 5–10 years plus with the same organization.

- This limited time window increases the urgency of developing individual athletes and teams in athletics as compared to the world of business. The urgency in athletics is also ratcheted up by the fact that coaches are limited by NCAA rules to a set number of hours with their team each week. In NCAA Division I women's volleyball, for instance, coaches are limited to 20 hours with their players during certain parts of the year, 8 hours during other parts, and are not allowed any contact whatsoever during the summer. In business, if you are preparing for a big presentation, you can spend as many hours as you like doing so.

- In business, there is typically a relationship between the age of your employees and the organization chart. As a broad generalization, 20-year-olds tend to report to 30-year-olds, who report to 40-year-olds, who report to 50-year-olds. But in athletics, head coaches work directly with players as well as their staff. So, a 40-year-old head coach will spend much of their day working with an 18-year-old. This spread of ages is rare in business.

- Most college athletic programs are committed to teaching life lessons in ways businesses are not. College athletes

are living away from home for the first time, are living in
a new place, and are adapting to the challenges of both
athletics and academics. They are not just developing as
athletes; they are developing as people.

- Most of the work in business is done behind closed doors
  and no one outside of the organization can see what is
  going well and what is not. On the other hand, the work
  of athletics takes place in the spotlight and is open to
  the public. Fans rate their team's and individual players'
  performance in real time with cheers and boos.

- Businesses have cross-functional teams that form as
  needed and disband once their work has been completed.
  The members of these teams are drawn from different
  parts of the organization, and may have never met each
  other before. Since the teams are temporary, they don't
  need to deal with every aspect of team building and
  conflict resolution. If you are not happy as a member of
  a team, just tough it out for three months and it will be
  over. In athletics on the other hand, though the team is
  refreshed annually with graduations and incoming first
  years, it never dissolves. Because of that, interpersonal
  relationships must be built and conflicts must be
  addressed and resolved.

- Finally, in athletics you have screaming fans, heckling,
  and standing ovations. In business, standing ovations are
  few and far between.

BETH'S REFLECTIONS ON THE BOOK

Beth has always dreaded becoming the seasoned coach who continuously talks about the way things used to be and how much

better it was in the old days. She never wanted to be a coach that uttered the phrase "Kids these days!"

Being a lifelong learner has kept Beth motivated even after 30 years in the profession. People ask her how she has been able to stay at one school doing the same job year after year. She tells them it has never been the same job. Every year has been different, and she is constantly looking for new and innovative ways to improve her coaching and design her program to win.

Coaching is about taking a group of individuals and forming them into a team. This is what she loves about the profession. There is so much that goes into the process of coaching that a neighbor of the late Carl McGown, who coached BYU to two NCAA men's volleyball championships and coached in seven different Olympics, said that coaching was more complex than his own job ever was. McGowan's neighbor was a rocket scientist.

Young coaches ask Beth, "How do I manage my staff?" This question comes up more often than any other. They do not ask her how she teaches the mechanics of volleyball as often as they ask:

- "How do I handle a staff member who is not loyal?"
- "How do I find enough time to organize my staff while still trying to coach my team?"
- "How long should I wait before deciding one of my staff members is a "C" performer and won't be turning things around?"

Five years ago, Beth decided to go outside the world of coaching and look for new answers to old questions. She had known Leo as a fan for years, but now their conversations became more substantial and intriguing. They would have a discussion, and Beth would keep coming back with more questions and ideas.

That questioning took her on the journey that led to this book.

Beth has always had systems in place to avoid reinventing the wheel. This has helped her efficiently answer the questions young coaches were continually asking her. She had been generous in sharing breakdowns of her staff's responsibilities, which, after 30 years, had become quite well developed. But, by digging deeper, she has continued to learn new ways to move her program forward and improve her understanding of what it means to be truly designed to win.

By applying proven principles and tools from outside her profession, she was able to see what was important and where she should be spending her time. Her biggest lesson was that everything that can be delegated must be delegated. This freed up her time to spend with her players on enhancing culture, on video and analytics, on donor relations, on recruiting, and most of all, on winning.

The concepts in this book can apply to many professions. Beth's excitement is that the book is at the intersection of business and sport. Her father was a small business owner, and she received her undergraduate degree in business administration and her master's in athletic administration. Business management has always been an interest for her, but it was the coaching profession that called to her.

Athletics invokes passion and is an important part of many people's lives. Studies show that, after their parents, coaches have the next highest level of influence on the lives of young athletes. Being a coach is an honored profession, and Beth feels fortunate to have been involved with the sport she loves for so long.

LEO'S REFLECTIONS ON THE BOOK

At the beginning, Leo looked upon his work with Beth as a fantasy camp. He had been a long-time fan, and it was a delight to peek under the hood of the coaching profession. But soon their discussions began refining the ideas he had been teaching and using with his business clients for more than three decades.

His clients began asking for copies of chapters long before this book had been published. When they asked, Leo always made it clear that the book is targeted at coaches and filled with sports examples. His clients have seen that as a benefit since they are looking to learn from the best-in-class in competitive knowledge and experience.

Leo had learned about as much as he was ever going to learn by applying his business concepts and tools to business situations. But his learning picked up again when he began applying those same concepts and tools to a different field of endeavor.

THE MAIN POINTS IN EACH CHAPTER

CHAPTER 1: THE PERFECT MATCH

- Having a program designed to win means not being surprised by success.
- Program victories come from both team and individual training, focus, and heroics.
- Your wins inspire others, both coaches and fans.

CHAPTER 2: WHAT IT MEANS TO BE DESIGNED TO WIN

- It is easy for management demands to take time away from coaching.
- A lasting vision statement anchors a program and lets everyone know what the program values while pursuing excellence.
- If you are designed to win and you work hard, success will follow. Even so, you will still have low points through which you must fight.
- You can choose whether you are a field mouse hiding from the predators or if you are the red-tailed hawk instilling fear into the hearts of your prey.
- A growth mindset is fundamental to being designed to win.
- Programs designed to win measure success in many ways.

CHAPTER 3: STARS AND "C" PERFORMERS

- Stars can impact your program in both positive and negative ways.
- You must push your stars to their full potential. Occasional failures are a necessary part of the process of doing so.
- The true cost of a "C" performer is far higher than you think.
- Though it is always easier to let a "C" player or staff member slide, programs that are designed to win deal with their "C's."
- The Left-Hand Column tool helps you hold difficult conversations that address the real issues.
- You must set high expectations for everyone, tailored to their individual strengths, weaknesses, and capabilities.

CHAPTER 4: THE POWER OF DELEGATION

- Anything that can be delegated must be delegated.
- You can't say "Yes!" until you learn to say "No."
- Your time has real value. Treat it as such.
- The leadership agenda clarifies high- and low-value uses of your time.
- "I can do it better and faster myself" is a terrible approach to getting work done.
- When you truly delegate a topic, it comes off your to-do list. When you kind-of delegate a topic, it stays on your list.

CHAPTER 5: CREATING ALIGNMENT BY USING GIVENS

- Givens enhance communication and align a program from top to bottom.
- Givens should be clear, explicit, and provocative.
- Higher-level givens are applied to all decisions within a program. Lower-level givens are relevant only for the specific decision for which they were created.
- Quality commitments enable accountability.
- Tasks and projects are different types of work and require different interactions between the head coach and the workers.
- Always tell less and know more.

CHAPTER 6: DEVELOPING EFFECTIVE STAFF MEMBERS

- Begin by developing your staffing philosophy.
- Manage your staff, but give them room to breathe.

- Giving effective feedback can be learned and must be practiced. Ask-Tell-Ask-Tell and SBI are helpful tools for giving feedback.
- The DISC tool (or other behavioral typing tools) helps staff and players communicate in ways that are effective for each individual.
- You will need to help your staff to stand up and be heard.
- Work/life balance is important and requires effort.
- You can never show too much appreciation to your staff.

CHAPTER 7: HIRING AND TRAINING YOUR STAFF

- Professionalism needs to be taught.
- Staff norms define the ground rules for how to work in your program.
- Case study interviews enable you to see how an applicant thinks.
- Being designed to win requires that you hire the best people, not just those who look, act, and think like you do.
- Developing an easily accessible knowledge storehouse helps you bring new people up to speed more quickly than starting from scratch. This is critical in the high turnover world of athletics.
- When you let staff go, it is a judgment based on their performance, not on who they are as a person.
- Your network is a powerful tool to help you and your staff obtain their next jobs.

CHAPTER 8: RECRUITING AND DEVELOPING YOUR PLAYERS

- You need to manage your talent pipeline.
- Establishing positional givens enables you to quickly screen out players who will not succeed in your program.
- Programs which are designed to win maximize both player and team goals and development.
- All players need to have meaningful roles that enable them to contribute to the overall success of the team.
- The Utah RED Chart allows you to visualize your entire program at a glance.

CHAPTER 9: DEVELOPING FANS AND DONORS

- Your program can have a profound impact on the lives of your fans.
- Better facilities enhance the fan experience.
- It is a coach's responsibility to build a fan base and foster donor relationships.
- Booster clubs bridge the gaps between fans and donors.
- The donor-centric model enables those who love your program to support it financially and get pleasure from doing so.

CHAPTER 10: CRISIS MANAGEMENT AND COVID-19

- The balance between formal vs. informal interactions was upset by the COVID-19 crisis.
- Crises are over-managed and under-led.
- There have been many crises before COVID-19, but they hit individual programs, not all teams at the same time.
- Maslow's hierarchy of needs provides guidance as to what should come first and what should follow during a crisis.

- COVID-19 is changing athletics, and it is not yet clear what the end game will look like.
- There are lessons learned from the COVID-19 crisis that will benefit programs when the world returns to a new normal.

CHAPTER 11: PREPARING FOR THE FUTURE

- The radar screen describes how the world is changing around you.
- Parts of your program are ready for the future, and other parts are stuck in the past.
- Identifying the trends going on around you enables you to identify necessary changes to keep your program relevant.
- Your program's rate of change is critical to its success.

CHAPTER 12: LEADERSHIP TIES EVERYTHING TOGETHER

- Coaching is both an art and a science.
- Leaders have a clear vision that guides their decisions and actions.
- Crafting your vision is best done using big blocks of time.
- You need to claim your place at the table as a leader.
- Data and connecting the dots are becoming increasingly necessary for excellent leadership.

HOW TO GET STARTED

Don't wait to apply the tools and concepts in this book until you understand them all. Don't try to apply all of the concepts at once. Don't wait to get your entire staff up to speed before taking action. Instead, start small and build. Find something which caught your imagination and give it a try. You don't have to do it perfectly on the first try.

We recommend a three-phase approach on the road to becoming designed to win:

Figure 13-1: Three-phase approach to becoming designed to win

Begin by proving the concept. Try some of the ideas in this book and prove to yourself that they make sense to you and that they work in your program. Among the best ways to begin are:

- Develop a list of givens for a task or a project.
- Create a leadership agenda and identify what is above your line and below your line.
- Practice telling less and knowing more in your next discussions.
- Ask questions of your staff first and wait for answers to get their true thoughts on a subject without your influence.

You may have other favorite tools and concepts you picked up from the book. If so, use those as your starting points.

Once you have proven the concept, build on success and apply additional tools and ideas. Bring others up to speed on what you are doing and the value you are seeing.

Finally, share your story. Begin with others in your program and introduce them to what you have been doing and the benefits you have realized. Then go beyond your program and share your successes with others. There is very little in this book that is specific to the sport of volleyball. There is very little that is specific to women's sports or men's sports. The ideas and tools we have introduced will benefit any team at any level.

CONCLUSION

The pairing of a business consultant with a Division I head coach may not have been an obvious match, but it has benefitted both parties. As professionals grow in confidence, capability, and experience within any one field, they move towards mastery of it. But eventually, their rate of growth slows because they have accessed the bulk of the ideas that make up the knowledge base in their field.

What seems difficult in one specialty may be routine in another because people in different specialties know different things. Leo would have no idea how to teach middle blockers serve-receive approach patterns to hit the gap or the slide, or transition footwork patterns to be able to attack in as many point-scoring situations as possible. That is simply not part of his experience or training.

Likewise, Beth would not know how to optimize the risk and return of a pharmaceutical research and development portfolio located in business units throughout North America, Asia, and Europe. What is the bread and butter of one specialty may be totally foreign to another.

On a humorous note, Leo had made a first cut describing a type of volleyball problem he would be clueless to solve. Beth saw it, laughed, and then totally revamped the example. Not only did Leo not know enough to solve the problem, but he also didn't know enough to describe a volleyball problem he couldn't solve.

The purpose of this book was not just to tell stories celebrating the career of a long-time coach. More importantly, we wrote it to show you that there are ideas not typically found in athletics that can be applied to your program to help you make the leap from simply competing hard to being designed to win.

If you have benefitted from reading this book, please rate and review it on Amazon or other bookselling sites. It is ratings and reviews from satisfied readers like you that convince others to pick up the book and begin the journey themselves.

To continue the conversation, please feel free to contact Beth at bethlauniere@gmail.com or Leo at teamhopf@gmail.com.